WORD MAGAZINE
presents

Reel Blak

Vol. 1: Guess Who's Comin' to tha Movies?

a pop culture guide to urban movies (post & pre hip hop)

D1283536

by

vanz chapman

50's: When famed showbiz publicist Walter Winchell was admonished by film critics of the era that Hollywood films should be more like real life, Winchell retorted: "On the contrary, it's real life that should be more like the movies."

60's: "He thinks you're going to faint because he's a Negro."

Reference to Sidney Poitier's character in
Guess Who's Coming To Dinner

70's: "[The movie] Superfly caused a fashion revolution. Overnight brothers went from Black Power Chic to Gangster Buffoon."

Nate McCall
Makes Me Wanna Holler

80's: "[Eddie] Murphy . . . the dapper child of the disco era . . . the smooth faced kid, takes over the screen, because he's playing black all the time. He's always calling attention to his blackness."

Pauline Kael
Taking It All In

90's: "And even after all my logic and my theory, I add a 'mothafuckah' so you ignorant niggahs hear me."

Lauryn Hill
The Score

Today: "The movie's [Baby Boy's] message to men like its hero is: Yes, racism has contributed to your situation, but do you have to give it so much help with your own attitude?"

Roger Ebert on
John Singleton's *Baby Boy*

to mom for that first book,
to kim for love and support,
to sam for being a dreamer,
for vanita for getting it started,
to russell, chris, ampora and alex
or their insight and a special thanx and
appreciation to ed, siri, naoko and sara
for their help

CONTENTS

Southern Discomfort

Lone Wolves

B-Boys & Gangstas

Black Docs

Our Planet Africa

Part 3: Enter tha Urban Cinematic Deconstruction Chamber

Tha Birth of a New Black Film Criticism

The Riffs and Rantz by vanz chapman & friendz
1.) Back in tha Day/Here & Now
  Beat Street
  The Show

2.) Girls Ain't Nothin' But Trouble
  Baby Boy
  Love & Basketball

3.) (White) Girls Ain't Nothin' But More Trouble
  Guess Who's Coming To Dinner
  Black & White

4.) Damn it Feels Good to be a Gangster
  Belly
  The Harder They Come

5.) (It was) da Best of Times and the Worst of Times
  Rappin'
  Wild Style

6.) I'm So Slack (Black Slackers)
  The Lunatic
  Basquiat

Appendix

Top Ten Best Urban Films
Top Ten Worst Urban Films
Top Ten Most Underrated Urban Films
Index of Films In This Book

Introduction: Where This Book Came From

Chicago - October, 2001

In the fall of 2001 I was flat broke. I had spent that year developing a TV series called *Lawd Have Mercy!* I'd forfeited most of my salary back into the development of the show in order for it to get done, and now I was feeling it.

And then in mid-October I was picked to go and be a FIPRESCI (International Federation of Film Critics) jury member for the new directors competition at the Chicago Film Festival, the oldest film festival in North America.

So with nothing but lint in my pockets, I was flown to Chicago, put up at a trendy four-star hotel, ferried around by request in a Mercedes M40 to screenings, and feted and fed at great restaurants nightly for ten days. Needless to say, it was a much-needed treat.

But something else happened that cool Chicago fall: As the only black film critic on the jury, it occurred to me during our discussions that over the years I had been digesting and interpreting films through my own culturally — and generationally-colored glasses. This wasn't a good or bad thing — it just was. Looking back at my take on black cinema over the last decade provided not just a chart of cinematic tastes but also of cultural and social changes.

The first half of Guess Who's Comin' to tha Movies? emerges out of that experience. The second half of this book comes from a more democratic place. While at the gym one day I overheard some 14-year-olds talking excitedly about the latest popcorn movie that had opened that weekend. This particular movie, panned by most critics, had left these kids thrilled by their viewing experience. As a film critic, one always wonders if anyone is listening — the tools of analysis that we use are not necessarily the ones that audiences use. The general public is not shackled by rules of criticism.

So I started to listen to what people in my diverse circle of friends were saying about movies. What they were saying was funny, insightful, and unique — the everyman's (and everywoman's) take. So in order to hold up a mirror to my "critical analysis" of black film I gathered these "consumer critics", the filmgoers who vote with their pocketbooks (people like sexual health counsellors and stand-up comics).

Together we broke down many of the films im-portant to our cultural generation, an opinionated ying to my analytical yang. What we achieved is well worth the effort.

Definitions

Bla(c)k film/movies: There's a famous scene in Spike Lee's film *Malcolm X* when Malcolm, just coming into some self-knowledge, looks up the word "black" in the dictionary. He sees that this word that is who he is is a dirty word: its definitions are full of negative connotations. It is then that he starts to realize what he's up against. Today the word "black", when used as a description of someone's ethnicity, is a loose description at best. You can be "black" and be from the West Indies or be "black" and be from the African continent or be "black" and be from the US. In this book we are also adopting the word's comprehensive qualities in our film classifications. We are deeming a film a "black film" if it's got a "black vibe", whether made by black filmmakers or not. For example, a black person does not direct *New Jersey*, but it's a black film, and the same goes for the *Rush Hour* movies. The films that we have dealt with in this book either have an actor or a quality that is of some interest or has some affinity with black culture.

Hip-Hop/Urban: Though this book deals with a variety of movies, the main focus of the book is on U.S. urban films from the '80s till now that deal either directly or indirectly with hip-hop culture. Sometimes the connection is immediate, sometimes not. For example the hip-hop documentary *The Show* deals directly with urban and hip-hop issues.

However a film like the '70s Jamaican classic *The Harder They Come* isn't about hip-hop culture per se but the themes about the urban underclass, gangsta culture, and music as a way of escape are most definitely echoed in the hip-hop themes and urban communities of today. So though the connections are not always readily apparent, especially with city-based films like *Salaam Bombay* or even *Pixote*, with closer observation the associations are there.

Part 1: Essays

The Patron Saintz of this Book

The following actors are two of the biggest and most important black movie stars of the hip-hop generation in the world today. Their characters are the ones that urban audiences always cheer for: our personal movie heroes that stand up to, rebel against, and comically outwit "The Man".

Culturally and creatively they embody the aspi-rations, charm, and sense of humour of urban culture: Will Smith, the boyish clown prince, and Chris Tucker, the quick-witted trickster. And as we embark upon a new era of moviemaking, they've both emblazoned the silver screen with powerful, zany, and riveting characters that, like all great cinematic stars, will be with us forever.

Chris Tucker: My Twenty Million Dollar Negro

Chris Tucker is the most important person in black cinema today. Why? 'Cause he's real funny? No. Because he's mad talented? He is, but no, that's not it. Chris Tucker is the most important person in black cinema today because his two box office hits, *Rush Hour* and *Rush Hour 2*, are the highest grossing films without a white male lead or co-star. That shit is nice.

Another cool thing about Chris Tucker is that he likes to tell it like it is. One of the first things that he says in my interview with him is about how he got into the twenty million dollar club (with *Rush Hour 2*) before Eddie Murphy: "Eddie just got in, right after me." And what's more amazing is that Tucker got only two million dollars to star in the original.

And like Tucker's new price tag, the sequel is bigger and badder as it has Tucker and Chan doing a little globetrotting. It opens with Tucker in Hong Kong for some R&R. Chan can't stop to hang with his boy as he's busy tracking down a leading mobster. When Chinese and US authorities begin fighting over jurisdiction of Chan's case, Tucker and Jackie decide to take global matters into their own hands. And off they go after international counter-feiters, triads, and shady American businessmen. They leave Hong Kong for LA and then on to a spectacular climax in Las Vegas.

But after sitting down to talk to Chris Tucker about his career, it's simple to see why he got the big money for this sequel — he honestly thinks he deserves it: "I know what my movies make so I should actually be gettin' fifty million." Chris chalks up the success of the films up to what he and Jackie both bring to the table: "Me and Jackie together bring great chemistry, great balance cause he has his fan base and I have a big [cross-over] fan base in America and we're just a mixture that people love."

So with Jackie Chan's global fan base and Chris Tucker's US urban fan base, *Rush Hour 2* aims to even outdo the box office success of the first one. Like the first movie, the sequel works because it basically sets up two kinds of scenes over and over: a scene for Chris Tucker to say something outrageous and act the fool, and a scene for Jackie Chan to unleash his brand of well choreographed ass whuppins. Chris loves to watch Chan's scenes: "Even if I'm not workin' that day, I'll come by the set just to watch him do his fight scenes." And Chris Tucker knows all of this, which is why he's not afraid to talk about doing as many sequels to *Rush Hour* as his fans want: "When I did Rush Hour, I thought it was a one-movie thing. I never thought it'd be a sequel, but once I got the chance to work with

Jackie again, I knew we could make something different, bigger, and better."

Rumor has it that *Rush Hour 3* has already been greenlit and will be set somewhere on the continent of Africa.

However, Chris' next film after *Rush Hour 2* is called *The Black President*. Chris loves to tell the story about meeting Bill Clinton on the set of the movie. It seems that the former Commander-in-Chief has a cameo in Tucker's comedy about the first black president of the United States, and Jesse Jackson, also on set, introduced Chris Tucker to Clinton. As the story goes, Jesse says, "Mr. Clinton, this is Chris Tucker. He's making a movie about being the first black president." Clinton then smiles, winks, and replies, "Tell him I already beat him to it."

Will Smith: The Skinny Kid from Philly Who Took On Ali

The first hip-hop rhyme I ever memorized was when Will Smith/Fresh Prince rocked the mic with the lyrics:

"Threw on my FILA underwear and my FILA hat, ran downstairs, and kicked the FILA cat."
—Jazzy Jeff and the Fresh Prince
Girls Ain't Nothin' but Trouble

Hardly deep stuff, but, over a decade later, people still remember Will Smith. It seems he's always been there — on the radio, on TV, on the big screen. And in a culture that quickly devours the flavor of the month and spits it out even quicker, Will Smith has done something that many superstars find hard to do — be around year after year.

So it's no surprise that Will Smith, the biggest black actor in the world, is about to play the biggest sports/cultural/political/sexual black figure of our time on the biggest stage in the world – the cinema. But he had to be begged to do it: "They [Ali's people] sent me a script and I thought it was great, but I thought, 'I can't play Ali.' He's the

13

greatest of all time. But then he called me and . . . I just knew that I had to give him the story that deserves to be told."

Indeed it is a story that deserves to be told. And while Hollywood finds time to turn out biopics on the likes of two-bit dope dealers (*Blow*) and two-bit porn stars (*Boogie Nights*), it's a shame that it's taken this long for Ali's life to come to the big screen.

But at least Hollywood seems intent on getting it right – Michael Mann is an exquisite director (*The Insider, Manhunter*), the budget has that magical hundred million dollar price tag to it, and Will Smith is a bona fide global superstar who's only going to get bigger. As a matter of fact, Will's gotten bigger already after having changed his body to play Ali: "Yeah, at this point I'm pretty gunned up. I'm 217 pounds, a good twenty pounds heavier than I've ever been, stronger than I've ever been." Will's physique is definitely a far cry from that of the skinny rapper from Philly, Def Jam's first rapper who wasn't from New York.

And like a pro, Smith parlayed rap stardom into TV stardom before jumping onto the big screen to save the world — twice. That's a task that's usually reserved for white guys. Now Smith is about to be larger-than-life once more.

Perhaps the success of the unearthed Ali documentary *When We Were King*s signaled to Hollywood that the public was ready to see Ali. Like Will Smith, Ali is an icon who has transcended race, class, and time, and ironically is probably the quintessential American icon.

What is more American than Ali's life? His sociopolitical trajectory soared through history. Born poor, he achieved wealth and fame in the true Horatio Alger mold. He represented the best of America when he won gold in the 1960 Olympics, and he detested the worst of America when he refused to fight in Vietnam. Ali married and divorced time and time again, eventually finding salvation in a higher power. He was a true loner.

Ali's life, with all its turbulence that was only weathered by a strong will, is what America is all about, or at least what they say it's all about. Why, he was even deified in that most American of media, comic books, when he took on Superman himself.

So here we are, forty years after Cassius Clay, a.k.a. Muhammad Ali, stepped into the collective ring of our consciousness with one of his trademark quick rhymes that, along with his quick fists, would make him one of the most famous people on the planet. Here we are, ready to accept him there again, this time via celluloid.

The man given the daunting task of being the vessel for the reincarnated myth of Muhammad Ali, a man that rocked heads inside the ring, is a skinny kid from Philly who used to rock the mic.

Da Nineties:
Hip-Hop and tha
New Black Aesthetic

"Too much of what we [black viewers] see seems too poorly defined."
   —Donald Bogle
   Blacks in American Films

"Are you a black painter?"
"No, I use other colors as well."
   —Basquiat

Years ago in the early 90s, at a social function held at the Smithsonian for lensman Arthur Jaffa (*Daughters of the Dust*), the respected D.O.P. reiterated something he had heard on the issue of the prowess of the black filmmaker. It seems that a professor in Boston had a theory that blacks had a "problem" with expressing themselves in terms of the pictorial. His reasoning was the fact that the main conveyance of African culture (stories/traditions) from one generation to the next was through the verbal form.

Unlike the European's affinity to have their art and culture written and sculpted, their African counterparts supposedly chose to have their records and art shared amongst one another in the fleeting and antivisual way of speech. Sadly enough, this theory seemed to make sense – poorly lit scenes, uncomfortable angles, and deathless composition couldn't always be explained away by the "low budget of black films" theory.

And though a film like *Chameleon Street* may have given black cinema its coolest, most complex, and intellectually challenging character ever — Doug Street — it might as well have been shot on video.

If kids in Brooklyn and the like could somehow go into a recording studio and construct beats, lyrics, and samples into such deft and infectious musical concoctions that even white kids in Italy would buy it, why wasn't there an equivalent in cinema?

The reason: Black musicians had succeeded in wooing the ears of the world because the language used in this art form was theirs, it was sincere, and it flowed from the soul. However, black filmmakers tried to tell stories with a cinematic language and alphabet that wasn't theirs. They tried to say things through the already established white structure, and it stank.

It's only the misleading appeal of nostalgia that makes most of these black films seem even remotely appealing (*Cooley High*, etc). If only somehow black visuals could be as funky as black beats.

During the last ten years, we've seen the usher-

15

ing in of the black aestheticians of medium and form. Spike Lee, arguably the point guard — so to speak — of postmodern black cinema hit the opening shot with *She's Gotta Have It*. Its success did much to debunk some of the myths that the "dinosaurs" of the established film industry had long perpetuated.

Everything from the big budget theory to Syd Field's much-followed, much- worshipped plot structure paradigm were reduced to the geocentric outdated concepts that they are. Spike, with a tiny 16mm arriflex camera and some black-and-white film stock, created an unlikely heroine in Nola Darling.

With a budget of less than a fifth of a million dollars, *She's Gotta Have It* went on to gross a staggering twelve million dollars. It made it possible for a film such as Hollywood Shuffle to find their way into cinemas across the country.

Though not classically trained like the NYU educated Spike Lee, filmmaker Robert Townsend nevertheless created an eternal classic with his quirky satire on black Hollywood. Though nowhere as visually deft (nor was it trying to be) as Spike's "joints," *Hollywood Shuffle* provided a painfully perceptive yet humorous metaphor of the absurdist theatre known as Black America.

At the height of the minstrel era, black performers, in order to be accepted by audiences would have to wear blackface (make-up) over whiteface over their black skin. A black man had to play a white man playing a buffoonish black man. The existential ramifications of such absurdity are eerie to say the least. *Hollywood Shuffle* is a feature length expression of such ramifications. With the likes of Spike Lee, Townsend, and Keenan Ivory Wayans getting Hollywood to open up its back doors, it wasn't long before the Afro-American cultural movement known as the Hip-Hop Nation gave birth to their own version of filmmakers that wanted in as well. By being able to mentally ingest everything from the politically articulate rage of Public Enemy to the adroit lyrical musings of brainy B boys De La Soul to the boastful southern bounce of the Outkast, the new young, gifted, and black generation of America brought a whole new take on the tricky concept of being black in America. It was paradoxically worshipped and crucified at the same time (i.e. Mike Tyson, Tupac, Biggie, etc.).

It was only a matter of time before the likes of John Singleton and the Hughes brothers would take form, filmmakers using hip-hop imagery to tell their stories. Singleton created a piece of cinema depicting a rite of passage so violently noble and bittersweet that audiences didn't know whether to cry in pity, scream in pain, or long to be part of that lifestyle. The Hughes brothers took it a step further. These music videomeisters told a similar story, but with the raw stripped-down style of early Scorsese. They gave a riveting glimpse of the nihilism that

America has created within the young black urban dwellers of the country. These films did away with the stereotypical monolithic "nightly news" version of the black gangsta and deconstructed their own version of the black gangsta to reveal the intricate inner workings of his mind and his world. It thus showed a far scarier image than the black thug being so for the sake of it. There's a complex method to the madness. In the words of Posdonus: "Fuck bein' hard, Posdonus is complicated."

Along with these changes there are rumblings being made by the female aspect of this new film movement. Audiences are ripe for the advent of a filmmaking Toni Morrison, Terry McMillan, or Alice Walker. Julie Dash, Cheryl Dunne, Gina Prince-Bythewood, and Euzhan Palcy do much to create powerful cinematic equivalents of the black woman's story as told by *Song of Solomon*, *Mama* and *Sweat*. More importantly, they will eventually give birth to a newer, cockier generation of black female filmmakers.

So while the likes of *House Party* made us roar at the buffoonery of Kid'n'Play, Spike's joints made us think, and Singleton and the Hughes brothers made us sit up and pay attention, they all served to prove one greater point: The black experience, in part due to the financial success of these films, is finally being allowed to be seen in some of its vibrant diversity. And the cottage industry of music video production continues to be a training ground for to-morrow's black filmmakers. More and more audiences will be treated to the sublime looking fables that former music videomeisters like F. Gary Gray, the Hughes Brothers, and Hype Williams churn out for the silver screen.

The new creators of black cinema have found their voice. They have also hit a universal chord. Black visuals are now as funky as black music. Just as the now critically dismissed "blaxploitation" era set the stage economically by showing Hollywood that there was a market for black movies and culturally by giving black audiences their own heroes, so, too, will the rap-influenced cinema of the 90s set the stage for the next black cinematic era.

Though the gangsta-rap-themed movies like *Boyz N The Hood*, *Menace II Society*, and *New Jack City* are now passé, they have inadvertently paved the way for the sexy black romantic comedies that are now deluging cineplexes everywhere. Films like *The Best Man*, *Two Can Play That Game*, and *The Brothers* owe their existence to the likes of Doughboy from *Boyz N The Hood* and Nino Brown from *New Jack City*: the bad boys who lived down the street, across the way.

Like their blaxploitation predecessors, hip-hop movie gangstas again showed Hollywood that a lucrative black movie-going public still existed. These movies not only showcased talent but also created an African American star system, which is what ultimately drives the movie system — people go to see Tom Cruise, not the story. This black star system allowed an actor like Morris Chestnut (*The Brothers, The Best Man*) to emerge as a sex symbol for the hip-hop generations and for an actor like Cuba Gooding Jr. (*Jerry Maguire, Snow Dogs*) to cross over into the mainstream. Both of these actors got their starts in the hip-hop gangsta flick *Boyz N The Hood*.

The important thing is that black cinema is no longer ghettoized. Hollywood is no longer just looking to green-light violent black movies. The black experience is now being screened in all its diversity, whether it be as superhero (*Blade, Blade II*), as romantic lead (*Two Can Play That Game*) or as cultural icon (*Ali*).

The collage of the different shapes, colors, and flavors of the black experience has always existed, and we've always known it. It's just nice to see it as such on the silver screen, lookin' so good.

Eminem & The Urban/Hip Hop Movie

Eminem's debut film, *8 Mile*, bum rushed theatres in the fall of 2002 and took in a staggering 55 million dollars, cash money, in its opening weekend. It had a per screen average of over twenty thousand dollars which is staggering; to put that figure in perspective, the nearest competitor in the top 10 that weekend had a eight thousand dollar per screen average. In the hip-hop world there was a collective sigh that could be heard in inner cities across the US. Once again, white artists capitalized on an African-American art form, much like rock and roll and jazz.

What makes this situation even stickier is that Eminem is a phenomenal lyricist. Even the most hard-core rap fan painfully, reluctantly and begrudgingly has to give Eminem his due: he's great.

But despite the genuine mic skillz that Eminem possesses it's obvious, and he even admits as much, that his record sales and immense popularity have as much to do with his bleached blonde hair and white skin as to do with his musical abilities.

After seeing the weekend grosses of Eminem's *8 Mile* and after reading the stream of accolades poured onto Slim Shady by entertainment writers from all over the country, I was reminded of a much less auspicious hip hop film debut 15 years ago.

In the late 80's when Run DMC released their groundbreaking album *Raising Hell* they were arguably at the apex of their popularity. Not only did they have the adoration and respect of the core hip-hop fan base, urban kids; they had a genuine crossover hit in their re-make of Aerosmith's "Walk This Way". Hip hop version of this rock classic made it's way from downtown to the suburbs where the white mainstream consumer started to take notice of this once underground culture.

Run DMC were also supposed to release a movie at the time of their 15 minutes of cross-over fame but legal issues prevented the movie, *Tougher Than Leather*, from being released until much later. And as any hip-hop fan knows, what's hot gets old real fast. By the time that the legal wrangling was over and the movie was released, Run DMC were no longer at the height of their popularity.

True, the Rick Rubin directed "neo-blaxploitation" pic that starred the group was by no means a great or even good film, but it's arguable that had the movie been released in the midst of the *Raising Hell* hoopla, that the film would have found an audience and become at least a cult hit. But with Run DMC's popularity in the wane, the flaws of the movie came off as bush league rather than charming.

Though NYC is the cradle of hip-hop civilization, the cultural petri dish where the music and lore of hip hop first took hold; it's never had a cinematic equivalent. The West Coast, with its G Funk addicted rappers like NWA, Snoop, and Warren G had cinematic dopplegangers in movies like *Boyz N The Hood, Friday* etc. — but NYC heavyweights like Tribe Called Quest and De La Soul never did.

Which brings us back to Eminem and how good or bad a film *8 Mile* really is. The story is trite, almost cheesy, but Eminem does have a great moody screen presence. The soundtrack slams. The black characters are genuine but they still adhere to the Hollywood rule that they exist only to aid the white protagonist rather than pursue their own dreams. Eminem's screen self is called B. Rabbit, an obvious play on the clever trickster character Brer Rabbit from the old southern Negro tales of Uncle Remus. But we don't know who's being tricked, black America or white America. In the end, despite Eminem's racy personae, the movie is pretty standard rags to riches stuff; it's Horatio Alger in a trailer park.

So why did it make 55 million dollars in its opening weekend? Is it 'cause he's white? Is it 'cause he sells a lot of records and that listening audience simply followed him from the record store to the cineplex? Or is he just stealing our shit and making money 'cause he makes Hip Hop safe for the lucrative, money spending, GAP wearing white suburban kid demographic?

The answer, like everything about Eminem, is

complicated. True, he sells a lot of records because he's a white boy, but it's also true that he's a better lyricist than a lot of top black rappers. True, the colour of his skin is why MTV gives him the red carpet treatment, but it's also true that he grew up just as poor and shit upon as many of his black, inner city counterparts; he does come from a single parent home, his dad did leave the family, Eminem does have a "baby mama".

But still the question remains, is Eminem legit? And that constant and lingering question is really what makes him more like his black "brothers" than anything else in his life. Because black America is what it is because of a similar question in all of its incarnations: are we smart enough, are we pretty enough, are we strong enough. This constant questioning of our being of our existence is exactly what Eminem endures as he flips the script and becomes a white man trying to make it in the black man's world. The spiritual resilience that is built up by constantly having to prove who you are is what ultimately makes Eminem an existential brother to Black America.

And it's what gives Eminem what he craves for more than record sales or heavy rotation on MTV: it gives him the respect of his peers and fellow artists.

UMWs - Urban Movie Watching Tools:

A Blaxploitation Primer

I have to confess that growing up, the appeal of blaxploitation films was always lost on me. Maybe it was because I didn't grow up in the US of A and thus couldn't appreciate these archetypal American style heroes that were reborn sepia toned on celluloid in the 1970s. After becoming a serious film critic I decided to take another look at the genre and try to get it. The three classics from that era that I took on were *Coffy*, starring the pneumatic Pam Grier, *Hell Up in Harlem*, starring Fred Williamson, and *Cotton Comes To Harlem*, starring Guyanese actor Godfrey Cambridge.

Hell Up in Harlem comes out swinging in the first few frames. It's pure testosterone. The film is actually a sequel to the equally violent *Black Caesar*, and it centres on the same main character. The plot is a mess of unmotivated action and cockamamie subplots involving formulaic crooked cops and double-crossing broads. But for all its faults, *Hell Up in Harlem* proves Godard's maxim about movies: If you got a girl and gun, then you got the makings of a movie.

Where Hell Up in Harlem is pure machismo, Coffy is pure jiggle. Coffy stars the queen of B-movies, busty siren Pam Grier, and as the poster of the day announced, "She's the baddest one-chick squad that ever hit town." The inconsequential script has to do with Coffy seeking revenge on the pushers and dealers who are responsible for her kid sister's addiction. But the real cinema in this movie comes while watching the gorgeous ex-Denver Bronco cheerleader single-handedly and single-mindedly "bring tha ruckus" upon the bad guys. And despite the criticism of black intellectuals, Gloria Steinhem put the image of this powerful black sister on her magazine cover. Right on.

One of the better blaxploitation films is Cotton Comes to Harlem, and it's probably no coincidence that it's one of the only blaxploitation pictures based on a novel. The novel, by under appreciated black author Chester Himes, follows the exploits of Himes' favourite characters — black detectives Coffin Ed Johnson and Gravedigger Jones, "Two detectives only a mother could love," says a movie poster for the film. Cotton Comes to Harlem was one of the first black films to combine action with comedy, and it holds up well to this day. Through this colorful romp through Harlem, we follow our heroes as they track down a missing $87,000. Chockfull of vibrant characters and high voltage action scenes, the true joy of the film is due to the sublime performances by the two great black actors — Raymond St. Jacques and Godfrey Cambridge — as the main characters. It is their underlying sense of nobility that gives this comedy its dramatic gravity.

So not till the summer of 1999 did I sit down and give blaxploitation films a real chance. Truth be told, I enjoyed them and understood their importance both culturally and artistically. First, it was simply for their absurdist appeal, but then more importantly, it was for the fact that these films possess an archetypal, albeit crude, good-against-evil morality machination beneath their cheesy veneer, and that is classic storytelling, black or white.

Pearl Harbor: A Whitesploitation Primer
or
"How White Guys Save the World 'Yawn' Yet Again"

What can I say about this "whitesploitation" classic? That it's a clever and insightful cinematic interpretation of a major historical turning point in modern global and cultural politics? That it depicts the end of innocence, the birth of the baby boomer, and yadda, yadda, yadda? Unless you're totally naïve, the film *Pearl Harbor* is none of these things. Nor could it be, and more importantly, nor does it want to be anything resembling intelligence and truth. Those two things don't exactly sell movie tickets.

Pearl Harbor is the latest mega-movie offering from supa producer Jerry Bruckheimer (*Top Gun, Con Air*) and supa director Michael Bay (*Armageddon, The Rock*). Armed with the largest film budget in Hollywood history, woulda-coulda- never-will-be movie star Ben Affleck, and the clout of the Disney studios, *Pearl Harbor* is out to be the blockbuster of the summer of 2001.

Will it be? Don't know. Is it a good flick? Hell no! And therein lies the problem. Like most big budget American films, *Pearl Harbor* looks good — real good. Jaw-droppingly good. Each shot is a stunning portrait of light and color. Each special effect is executed to perfection. The musical score is exquisite (in that over the top nauseating way). The stars — Ben Affleck, Kate Beckinsale, and Josh Hartnett — are photographed with such precision that they look like, like, the most beautiful human beings, like, ever.

Does the movie suck? Hell yes! Is it a bad movie? No. Why? 'Cause a movie is made up of many things: story, performance, technique, luck. The craftsmanship of *Pearl Harbor* is beyond reproach. But after an hour and a half of watching it, I wanted to leave. I was that bored, but I was also fascinated of how well the film was put together up onscreen.

Do I know anymore about this important historical event after having seen the film? Hmm. Well, I know that. . . that. . . actually I think I know less about the real *Pearl Harbor* after having seen the film than before.

Are the battle sequences as amazing as they say? Hell yeah! I could talk about the laughable historical inaccuracies. I could ridicule award-winning black actor Cuba Gooding Jr. for taking such a nothing role, in such a nothing movie with almost no screen time. I could tell you how the scenes involving the Japanese military strategist play with such straight-up exposition that they might as well have had the screenwriter just get on camera and explain to us the what, why, and where's. It was that bad. I could do all of that. But I won't.

What was my favorite part of the movie? The part when Alec Baldwin shows up in the third act as Capt. Doolitle, the real-life heroic pilot who led a morale boosting bombing run on Tokyo in the wake of the Pearl Harbor attack. He's so unintentionally funny and over the top that I think he was doing it on purpose. I might actually sit through that three-hour behemoth again just for those laughs alone.

The Chasm between Black Male Filmmakers and Black Female Writers

"I am a black woman...defying place, time and circumstance...look on me and be renewed."
   —Mari Evans
   I Am a Black Woman

"Cancel that bitch. I'll get another one."
   —Nino Brown
   New Jack City

As a student at a black university in southern Virginia back in the 90s, I remember the parade of black cultural figures that came through our auditoriums, mostly writers and mostly women. One afternoon, while listening to Nikki Giovanni bash the Afro-American male, it occurred to me that there were not many, if any, black male counterparts to refute or challenge the barrage of accusations hurled by the likes of Nikki Giovanni, Alice Walker, and Terry McMillan. In that auditorium I could feel, see, and hear the absence of a Black Male Cultural

Critic. For every negative observation given by these talented women writers there should have been a male voice trading barbs with it. Instead, all we got was a lopsided, one-sided dialogue.

During the late eighties and early nineties, the advent of the new black cinema gave us the opposite. The media chose to focus on black male filmmakers and their stories even though independent black female cinema has had, and continues to have, its visionaries (Zeinabu Davis, Julie Dash, Euzhan Palcy).

And in a media saturated society, what gets reported is what exists. Cries of misogyny were heard up and down the aisles as poorly defined and often degrading images of black women were offered up in the expressions of this new black (male) cinema. The same accusations of woman hating were simultaneously directed at the blatant anti-female sentiments often touted in many rap songs. Again, one-sided dialogue.

The popular black filmmakers and the popular black rappers were giving their observations (insults?) on the black woman, but there were few, if any, female artists in either field to counter these artistic attacks. What were, or are, the reasons for this squaring off in different artistic arenas?

The culture of the African oral tradition is common to both men and women. However, women have taken to the solitary solace of the written word to express the complexities and absurdities often facing black women and have dominated the writer's landscape. Alternately, men have seized on the spoken word and fashioned it into a vivid and funky linguistic tool to blare their story to anyone that would listen.

So with much of the new black cinema (*House Party, Do The Right Thing, New Jack City, Tales From The Hood, CB4*) being another manifestation of the male-dominated hip-hop culture and the unfavorable light that black women writers still like to shine on black men – a black male journalist once stated that Alice Walker has made a living off of degrading black men – the rift and chasm between these two groups of artists serves as a sad metaphor for the strained relationship between the individual black man and woman in society.

When Alice Walker whipped up the motley and unsavory crew of male characters in her classic *The Color Purple*, black men cried foul. However, when Wesley Snipes' *New Jack City* character Nino Brown gripped his "lady," doused her with champagne, and told his henchmen, "Cancel that bitch. I'll get another one," the male audience giggled with glee. Two voices, borne from the same myriad of emotion and experience, separated, not to compliment one another but rather to tear at each other, and in effect, tear at themselves.

Hopefully with new black female filmmakers like Gina Prince-Bythewood (*Love & Basketball, Disappearing Acts*) flexing their cinematic skills, and gangsta films having given way for male-themed romantic flicks like *Two Can Play That Game*, not to mention the emergence of sensitive black male writers like Trey Ellis (*Platitudes, Home Repairs*) and E. Lynn Harris (*Invisible Life*), the two mediums will become more gender-balanced, and finally we will have that dialogue that our community so desperately, desperately needs.

Losing My Cherry:

Covering a Film Festival for the First Time — Toronto International Film Festival Planet Africa, 1994

The first time that I ever turned a critical eye to the layers, subtext, and narrative structure of black movies was during the 1994 Toronto International Film Festival (TIFF).

As a neophyte film critic, one of my first assignments was to cover and review several of the black films that were shown at the festival. Having been educated at black universities in the States, I had been heavily and seductively influenced by US urban culture — the hip-hop generation. So after having a steady cinematic diet of everything from *She's Gotta Have It* to *Boyz N The Hood* to *CB4*, I was looking forward to seeing what black film artists from the rest of the black diaspora were saying along with their African-American counterparts.

Variety is the spice of life, and that is precisely what was most enjoyable about the selection of black films (themes or otherwise) back then at that TIFF 1994. They were just that — a selection, a cinematic smorgasbord, a variety of black-issued films that gave the audience several idiosyncratic glimpses into the world of different shapes and flavors that the black experience and black narrative comes in.

Though the offerings were somewhat sparse, they were nevertheless delectable. Akin to a nouvelle cuisine meal, the portions, while small, were a worthwhile experience. The films also touched on several issues and themes ranging from the absurdity of the American dream as seen through the eyes of two young inner-city basketball players trying to make it to the pros to the psycho-dramatics of American filmmaker Charles Burnett's thriller *The Glass Shield*. There was also the feminism and femininity of Canadian filmmaker Selina William's *Saar,* the biting West Indian satire of Isaac Julien's *The Darker Side of Black* and finally, the humorous complexities of growing up black in hostile, foreign post-war England as shown in Alrick Riley's moving *The Concrete Garden*.

***

Hoop Dreams

"I'll never let another serve me, I'll get flyer than that [#] 23 on Mr. [Michael] Jordan's jersey."
—Das Efx

Hoop Dreams is a collaborative three-hour documentary by Steve James II, Frederick Marx, and Peter Gilbert that spans four and a half years of the lives of two black high school basketball players in Chicago. Critics have called it one of the most important and precise portraits of the American experience, and what is interesting about that statement is that it does not differentiate between the American experience and the Afro-American experience, which is almost always done, sometimes for good cause.

The stranger-than-fiction documentary follows thirteen- and fourteen- year-olds Arthur Agee and William Gates from being "spotted and captured" by a local adhoc scout from a prestigious private school all the way to their first year in college. At the beginning, in a scene reminiscent of some old slave-catching scenario, William and Arthur are scooped from their respective inner-city playgrounds and whisked away to the legendary halls of St. Joseph's, an expensive private school known for its basketball program.

At first glance the story seems to be simply about the trials and tribulations of hard work in sports, but it soon becomes more – much more. It becomes a bittersweet, ironic, touching, nervy, eloquent, insightful story, and a true story at that, about life and all its layers, about America and all its dreams, about boys as they kick, scream, drift, and charge into manhood before our very eyes.

In a plot line that the best screen hacks in Hollywood couldn't come up with, both Arthur and William are given scholarships to the prestigious private school, a three-hour trip away from home. The school is a known stepping-stone to the big basketball universities which themselves are heartbeats away from the pros. So the two jump at the opportunity.

Isiah Thomas, St. Joseph's claim-to-fame alumni, appears in the film talking to the kids whilst in basketball uniform with a ball in hand. The image is demeaning and seems to strengthen the "blackman as ball player" stereotype. However, a little later in the film Spike Lee appears in an ever-so-brief, yet riveting scene, admonishing the kids to be smart about their futures and not to be taken advantage of by big-school ball.

While at St. Joe's, William grows bigger and stronger, and embraces the program; Arthur remains small and at odds with the coaching. In a shady turn of events, Arthur is asked to leave the school because of the "financial shortcomings" of his family. From here, this tale of two boys takes on a bizarre, almost surreal sense of duality as William becomes a beneficiary of the financial favours of a local business woman/friend of the schools, while Arthur is forced to enroll in a dilapidated inner-city public school.

His mother then loses her job, and they have to go on welfare. In an ironic set of scenes Arthur's family is eating dinner in a dark apartment because they can't afford electricity, while William is in a bright, high-tech clinic being inserted into a humming sonographic chamber in order to "check his knees". It is a scene indicative of the absurdities of life in America.

Poetically though, it is Arthur who galvanizes his underdog, public school team and leads them to the "big game downstate."' while William and his prep school team fail to even make it to the playoffs. In a sincere, heartfelt moment, Arthur comes to watch William's final losing game, and the camera catches them in an emotional embrace, after the heartbreaking loss and years after the two were discovered on the playground.

It's apparent that the film would not have been as effective if it were only about these two lives in and around the court. It works because it shows the anatomy of life up-close and personal. For example, we see Arthur's father become addicted to cocaine, leave the family, rehabilitate, return, and leave again. In William's case, we see him become a teenage father intent on raising his family as a man, unlike his own father.

The number of literally fantastic moments captured on film are too numerous to mention and the "plot" too quirky to explain, but most importantly, the film has managed to grasp the oft fleeting moments that constitute a dream.

***

The Darker Side of Black

"Pity the nation divided into fragments, each fragment deeming itself a nation."
— Kahlil Gibran

The other documentary in this selection, Isaac Julien's *The Darker Side of Black*, takes a more witty and satirical stance towards its subjects. Julien takes a close unblinking look at homophobia in the black, mostly-youthful subcultures of dancehall and hip-hop. With Arthur Jaffa's (*Crooklyn*) distinctive and dreamy lensing, Julien attempts to delve into the collective black psyche as it pertains to homosexuality, a subculture within a subculture. His camera takes us from macho posturing interviews with hip-hop cultural mega-star Ice Cube to sincere observations from the Brand Nubians to intimate foot-in-mouth interviews with Shabba Ranks

and Buju Banton. This main narrative is peppered with peeping-tom glimpses into raunchy dancehall parties, as well as rebuttal rhetoric from the likes of a staunch Jamaican theologian and even a former Jamaican prime minister.

Isaac Julien, an openly gay filmmaker, makes a skillful attempt to indict and sometimes even ridicule the attitudes that perpetuate violent homophobic sentiment. However his intent is sometimes undermined by the very weapons he uses to make his points: the lush slowed-down clips of hip-hop videos at times prove to be more seductive than disturbing.

Julien's attempt to provide Banton with just enough rope (film time) to hang himself during their interviews sometimes backfires. Buju is a star, and like most stars, he possesses a considerable amount of charisma and charm. The camera captures this, so at times we are taken by him rather than repelled.

Overall though, Isaac Julien has produced an insightful, critical vision of a sad rift within the black community that unfortunately puts up more barriers within a community that should be seeking cohesion rather than separatism.

***

Saar

"Singing little brown woman, singing strong black woman, singing tall yellow woman...for you all I have many songs to sing... could I but find the words."
—Langston Hughes

Every so often, the pen is subtly able to capture in words a beauty and gentleness of expression that can be often only experienced in the actuality of the moment or moments. And even less often, the camera is able to capture an effective visual interpretation of the words. Such are my feelings towards Selina Williams' *Saar*.

A 'saar' is an African emotion-cleansing ritual. Selina has aptly chosen this word as the title for her film that poignantly celebrates the coming together of six different Afro-Canadian women, each with different ideals and even differing sexualities. They gather together one night to enjoy food, music, warmth, spirituality, and most importantly, themselves. Selina cleverly throws into this mix of positives a constant, nagging negative in the form of broadcasted reports of the death of young Somali boy at the hands of a Canadian "peacekeeper". This serves to illustrate the dichotomy that being black in a foreign country creates. It also serves to instigate discussion and emphasize the consciousness of these women.

The short starts weakly and the acting slightly uneven, but the narrative and performances soon bloom into an eloquent articulation of the beauty and resilience of the female aspect of the Afro-Canadian experience. The cinematography revels in all the lush hues that their African skin has to offer, and the images that Selina chooses to linger on – a crackling fire, a lock of hair – speak volumes.

The spiciness that the coming together of these positive sisters is bound to evoke keeps the pacing edgy and necessarily bitchy. The short poetically and humorously ends with each of the women metaphorically freeing themselves of, among other things, "tired brothers".

Amen.

***

The Glass Shield

"Doctor! Always do the right thing."
—Da Mayor
Spike Lee's *Do The Right Thing*

Charles Burnett's morality tale *The Glass Shield* has been called his most traditional film to date. Though this film does follow a more standard story path than we usually see from Burnett and the characters are somewhat stock, the film is nonetheless infused with the complex moral dramatics that we know Burnett will provide in a film.

The Glass Shield focuses on JJ, an idealistic young black police officer fresh out of the academy. His first placement is at an all-white, tough, racist precinct in Edgemar, California. Here, JJ does his best to serve and protect and play by the rules. He even adheres to their "sticking together no matter what" policy, even if it infringes on truth itself.

Later in the story, a young black man, Ice Cube, is pulled over by one of JJ's fellow officers for no reason other than the color of his skin. A gun is found in Ice Cube's car and though it belongs to his girlfriend's father, the racist police machinery plots to make him the fall guy for the unsolved murder of a white woman. The only thing that can stop the trial from going forward is if JJ truthfully admits that Ice Cube did not commit the traffic violation that his police colleague claims is why he pulled

the car over in the first place. JJ chooses to lie for the force. The jaws of the legal machinery are now poised to swallow another innocent young black man. It is not until JJ's fiancée and local community leaders help him realize the magnitude of what he's done that he breaks down and does the right thing.

At its most basic, Burnett's film is an action thriller about a good cop at a bad precinct. However, at work within this surface narrative are a host of other complexities.

The racist agenda of the crooked precinct as a backdrop to JJ's loyal black cop is a sad ironic metaphor for the situation of a lot of blacks in the States: it's modern day Sisyphus. One scene in which an attractive black woman motorist is slightly harassed by JJ's white partner after JJ had earlier let her off with a warning speaks volumes about unfairness. The shots of the woman's blinking eyes in her rear view mirror as she hopelessly looks at her powerless "brother" is absolutely moving though no words are spoken.

The various subplots of community activism, courtroom dramatics, insurance scams, and a dying police detective are handled rather pedestrianly, but Burnett is more concerned with the bigger, deeper issues, and it shows.

Finally, the darkly ironic plot twist towards the end that somehow leaves JJ as the sole scapegoat in this rotten web of deceit brings to mind a line from the hip-hop group Brand Nubians:

Now, here's some food for thought,
Many fought for the sport
But the black man still comes up short.

***

The Concrete Garden

"I was now in another world, a world which grew into many worlds and engulfed me, though something of me was always separate and belonged to the beautiful green hills of my childhood."
—Claude McKay

The last course on our cinematic menu is Alrick Riley's *The Concrete Garden*, a skillfully made short narrated in the form of letters from a young West Indian girl in England to her grandmother back in the islands. Riley's story of this young girl's first experiences in the UK serves as a moving example of the many tales of isolation that all young immigrants face in some degree. *The Concrete Garden* manages to be humorous and noble all at once. The scenes that follow the young heroine from a farewell gathering in her sunny home to a cold and lonely "non-reception" at a train station in the UK smartly strikes the visual and emotional contrast

that she goes through. At school she is terrorized by a couple of menacing yet somewhat absurd white girls in an immigrant rite of passage. This is followed by a sweet moment where the young girl's younger brother hands her a roll of tissue for her bloody nose. He, too, knows the new kid "black and blues."

The last that scenes involve the protagonist,s attempts to sneak into a nightclub and see her musical idol perform are comic but heavy-handed. Despite that, the film is cleverly perceptive and very enjoyable.

***

Back in the Days

As an after-dinner sweet, Dewey Thompson's *Back in the Days* was aptly short and sweet, sort of bittersweet. The three-minute short is a surreal dreamy sequence of a young black boy who magically kills a white businessman in the building across from his.

In a weirdly interesting image, the young boy marches through the tree-lined streets of the white man's suburban neighborhood. He drifts through the now fatherless home and finds the man's car keys. It seems "he won't be needing them," the youngster muses. In a fitting and (somewhat) disturbing climax, the boy matter-o-factly takes the car and goes to "look for my father."

***

CRITICAL CONCLUSIONS

And so went my introduction into 'serious' film criticism. Though I had done film reviews for the student paper *The Hilltop* while I was a student at Howard University, during the Festival that year I felt that I became a film critic in the real sense of the term. The eclectic and well-rounded group of black voices that spoke to me in those darkened cinemas that sweltering summer were not only beautiful on their own, but their true mesmerizing melodious appeal was in the way that all these different tones that these different "black" films achieved, complimenting each other to the point that together they formed a symphonic and unifying voice and feeling.

Now going into the double-0s (2001, 2002, 2003) and after having covered the Toronto Festival for the last eight years as well as others and the occasional made-for-TV movie, I find myself ready to re-examine some of the films that emerged during the last decade and a half. They not only influenced me as a writer and critic, but they also influenced my generation, the hip-hop/post-hip-hop generation.

Just like a scientist, a hip-hop music producer will use beats and melodies from the 50s and 60s as a counterpoint to their present day lyrics and arrangements to create an amalgam of then and now, and so will Guess Who's Comin' to da Movies? 'Cause we, too, are seeking to critically sequence the films of the hip-hop generation and their cinematic forebears that gave birth to them in order to illustrate the socio-cultural genealogy between "back in tha day" and "here and now."

Part 2:
Reviews
Black Film in the 90s

Or

(A Critical Diasporic Journey through Black Cinema during the Clinton Era)

The following reviews are in the tense (past, present, etc.) that they were originally written in order to maintain the immediacy of the take on the film at the time of it's release and not revised in any retrospective tone.

During the Reagan/Bush 80s, something amazing happened to black America on the cultural front: Quincy Jones, Vibe magazine hit the newsstands, Bill Cosby was the biggest TV star in the world, Eddie Murphy was the biggest movie star in the world, Spike Lee was the most dangerous filmmaker in the world, and David Dinkins was about to be mayor of the biggest city in the world. More importantly, kids from New York City unleashed hip-hop culture unto mankind. A cultural movement that would go on to affect how everyone on this planet would talk, think, and be.

But despite all these changes, black film still hadn't hit its stride. The number crunchers in Hollywood had yet to discover the lucrative black cinema-going market, so much so that studios would not release black films against each other during the same opening weekend. The reasoning was that the public wasn't ready for 'choice,' that this audience would only spend their dollars on one film.

Then Spike Lee came and made loot. Like emotionally-starving stepkids, inner city audiences were going to see Spike's films two and three times apiece, an economic phenomenon known in Hollywood as 'return audience," a rare occurrence even for the biggest summer blockbuster.

So Hollywood not only started making 'black' movies en masse, they also started to release/distribute a variety of black-themed independent films and even documentaries to feed this new market. And at the very least, they started casting black actors in roles that were originally written for white actors. In doing so, they sometimes made that film into a black movie. What follows is an in-depth sampling of many of those films — eat up!

BLACK POPCORN MOVIES

Bad Boys

Directed by Michael Bay
Starring Will Smith and Martin Lawrence

Take two popular afro-sitcom comics, pose them in front of the neo-mod backdrop of glam and mon-eyed Miami, set in motion a done-to-death, hi-tech, shoot 'em up drug plot, throw in the slimmest of twists so that the audience feels as if they're thinking, and — by George! — it works. Despite what detractors say, raunchy Martin Lawrence plays well off of Will Smith's GQ-Negro-next door turn to provide some genuine chemistry amidst the gorgeous Miami setting.

The too-quick-to-think plot about the heist of some drugs from a police lockup and the two street savvy cops (Lawrence and Smith) who have to crack the case is well worth the video rental fee. With its wide screen, smokin' colors, and swirling camera, *Bad Boys* provides a wicked cinematic ride. Some of the subplots (like Will and Martin having to switch identities) are hair-brained, but so what? This film has all the elements that draw mainstream audience into the cinema in droves.

After raking in over sixty million dollars at the domestic box office, a *Bad Boys* sequel is in the works, and the big screen stock of both these actors has increased by several zeros. (Lawrence made three million on his next picture.)

***

Big Momma's House

Directed by Raja Gosnell
Starring Martin Lawrence and Nia Long

Martin Lawrence movies are like kids, movies in that they're critic-proof. If you like Martin Lawrence, you're gonna go and see the movie, and you're gonna laugh, no matter what the critics say.

That being said, *Big Momma's House* is not bad, just extremely formulaic. The director, Raja Gosnell, was the editor of *Mrs. Doubtfire*, the Robin Williams-in-drag smash hit comedy so Raja has obviously taken a page from that book: What's funnier than a funny comedian? A funny comedian in drag as an old woman. Like most movies in this "genre", the plot is fairly non-existent.

Instead, we just set up scenes to let Martin do his thing in the granny suit. Granny schoolin' some bullies on the basketball court, Granny drop-kicking a smart-ass karate instructor, Granny gettin' the spirit in the local church, and the beat goes on.

The filmmakers are savvy enough to show just how luscious Nia Long can be. They even manage to get her into some sexy lingerie that just about gives Big Momma a heart attack.

The story sets up Martin as a master-of-disguise FBI agent who goes undercover as a southern 'fried' cantankerous Grandma. His mission is to befriend a young woman whose boyfriend has just escaped from prison and is looking for two million dollars that she may be hiding.

Unlike Lawrence's last film, slicker-than-slick *Blue Streak*, *Big Momma's House* lets Martin show off his sweet side both as Big Momma and as the alter ego FBI agent. Martin even gets the girl and a sincere onscreen kiss in the end.

So despite the cookie cutter feel of the movie, Martin's showmanship and the sheer joy of performance that he exudes shines through the dreck of the cheesy script, and it makes the movie worth seeing.

***

Brown Sugar

Directed by Rick Famuyiwa
Starring Taye Diggs and Sanaa Lathan

'I met this girl when I was ten years old, and what I loved most was she had so much soul.'
—Common
"I Used To Love Her"

When the rapper Common used the archetypal "boy meets girl" theme as a metaphor for the ups and downs that the hip-hop generation had gone through, it became an instant classic. It captured perfectly the tumultuous relationship that we all had with the ever-changing music and culture of hip-hop. Now writer/director Rick Famuyiwa has skillfully used that same theme as a backdrop to his sexy urban love story *Brown Sugar*. The movie stars heartthrobs Taye Diggs and Sanaa Lathan as best friends who grew up in love with hip-hop only to discover that they're really in love with each other.

As is evidenced in his debut film *The Wood*, Famuyiwa again knows how to play to the nostalgia that hip-hop heads are starting to feel for the purer early days of the music. And now the characters, like hip-hop itself, have grown up, matured, but inevitably lost their way. Set in the birthplace of hip-hop, New York City, *Brown Sugar* gives us Taye Diggs as Dre, a successful but unfulfilled record exec, and Sanaa Lathan as his best friend Sidney, a successful music critic. Like all good love stories, as soon as we see them we know they're meant to be together. Unfortunately, they don't. As a matter of fact, Dre gets married to an uptight lawyer, and Sidney gets engaged to a meathead ball player before they realize what's up. After Dre and Sidney have their required epiphanies, the two reluctant love birds finally find their way into each others' arms (and beds). Along the way Queen Latifah pops up as comic relief, playing Sidney's loud-mouthed girlfriend, and Mos Def is a no-nonsense MC featured in a sub-plot involving the ongoing battle between good and bad rap music.

All in all, *Brown Sugar* is amazing with sleek cinematography, a hittin soundtrack of new school hits and old school classics, and everyone looking stunning and beautiful. It's just the way a love story should be.

***

Dr. Dolittle

Directed by Betty Thomas
Starring Eddie Murphy

In his film *48 Hours*, Eddie Murphy boasted to a bar full of rednecks that he was "your worst nightmare — a nigga with a badge," and it was lines like that with which Murphy announced himself to filmgoing audiences. Despite the facade though, it was obvious that Murphy's "take-no-prisoners" shtick was just that — "shtick" — but at least it was fun watching him "sticking it to whitey".

However, now he has taken the all-too-familiar route that a lot of cutting edge comedians take — the route that allows the artist to reinvent himself into a wholesome family friendly icon. Someone who can be plugged into classic, tried-and-true formulaic vehicles to hoover cash from kids and parents alike every summer. Murphy did it with *The Nutty Professor*, as did Robin Williams with *Flubber*. Both films inexplicably grossed over two hundred million dollars each.

This summer Murphy pulls up to the screen in the Twentieth Century Fox vehicle, *Dr. Dolittle*, a contemporary remake of the 1967 classic that starred Rex Harrison and features the now classic song "Talk to the Animals." But this film is a remake the way that Puff Daddy's "Missing You" is a remake of the Police classic "Every Breath You

Take." It's a very loose translation. That being said, audiences know what they're going to get, and I'm sure they'll show up in droves to see Eddie be Eddie — which is what Murphy does best. Like most big budget Hollywood fare, the film is technically beyond reproach with top notch cinematography and production design and a bumping r&b/hip-hop soundtrack which provides funky beats to accompany the action.

With a running time of less than ninety minutes, the soundtrack helps the film move quickly. Murphy plays Dr. Dolittle, an overachieving San Francisco doctor who has just reached the pinnacle of professional success. His practice is about to be bought out by a corporation with deep pockets in a deal that will make him rich. Unfortunately his family situation is not riding on a similar high. In typical 90s fashion, the good doctor is self-involved, and he's no Dr. Huxtable to his two little daughters and his gorgeous wife.

But once Dolittle's ability to talk to the animals returns to him, after being exorcised decades earlier when he was a child, the fun begins. A scruffy street mutt ingratiates himself into Dolittle's life and becomes his sidekick during the adventure. Norm Macdonald voices Lucky the pooch with droll one-liners. Things kick into overdrive when the animal kingdom hears about Murphy's "gift," and they bumrush his condo. Dolittle's house is overrun by a menagerie of animals looking for treatment for a variety of problems, including a drunken French circus monkey who can't put down his tiny bottle of Jack Daniels.

The cookie-cutter climax is set up when Dolittle finds out that the tiger from the circus in town needs surgery. Dolittle ends up kidnapping the tiger and performing emergency surgery after the prerequisite soul rediscovery scene with his daughter. And voila, the day is saved, and the good doctor goes on to treat both animals and people in his practice.

If the comedy seems broad, it is, but so is most family movie fare. The kids will go nuts for the smart-mouthed animals, particularly John Leguizamo's ungrateful rat and Chris Rock's zany guinea pig. And there is just enough of Eddie's more adult antics to provide the parents with sufficient chuckles.

***

Dr. Dolittle 2

Directed by Steve Carr
Starring Eddie Murphy

Dr. Dolittle 2 is one of those rare sequels that is actually better than its predecessor. The original Eddie Murphy *Dr. Dolittle* played like an average Disney Sunday night TV-movie, mostly because it seemed like Eddie didn't even wanna be in the movie 'cause he couldn't swear and couldn't do his "angry Negro" shtick. But the movie made close to three hundred million at the box office and sold millions more of the soundtrack. Fortunately, in *Dr. Dolittle 2* Eddie seems to have gotten a better grasp on this whole wholesome-family-entertainment thing.

The film opens in the same stunningly beautiful San Francisco neighbourhood as the first *Dr. Dolittle*. The doctor is now a minor celebrity, a sort of animal Dr. Joyce Brothers/Dr. Ruth. Things are going smoothly for the doctor and his picture-perfect family until his oldest daughter starts experiencing some severe growing pains that threaten to pull the family apart and in the midst of that, the animal mafia makes the good doctor "an offer he can't refuse."

It seems that a Disney-esque evil corporation wants to tear down a local forest, which would leave countless animals homeless. Dr. Dolittle is called upon to save the day by a beaver, the Godfather of the forest. The story is serviceable, though you can see plot developments unfolding a mile away and the underlying Greenpeace-like message is blatant pandering, but the joy is in the performances. Eddie Murphy is the funniest he's been in this sort of role and the talented voices that he gets to play off make for some good comedy.

And having his eldest daughter (excellently played by Raven Symone) go through her first crush during the doctor's crisis puts Eddie in such a manic state that it serves the narrative well. Having to deal with animal neuroses and his daughter's raging hormones is a great comic mix.

The bulk of the comedy is derived from the plan that the doctor comes up with in order to save the forest: if he can prove that a rare bear species is "making baby bears" in said forest, then the forest will be spared. The only problem is there's only one such bear in the forest, and she's female, and the only other such male bear for miles around is Archie — a wacky, neurotic circus bear. You get the picture.

It's up to Eddie to teach this city bear how to be a country bear and Eddie tries everything from throwing Archie into "bear jail" to toughen him up to trying to demonstrate how to walk like the alpha male. Needless to say, all these attempts hilariously fail, with ridiculous visual punch lines.

In the end, it all works out, of course. The bear gets the girl, Eddie gets his family back, and the forest is saved. *Dr. Dolittle 2* could easily be picked apart for a bunch of narrative and performance flaws, but in a way it reminded me of the great Disney farces like T*he Love Bug, World's Greatest Athlete*, and *The Computer Wore Tennis Shoes* that I loved as a kid. Sure they're dumb in a lot of ways, but that's the point.

***

From Hell

Directed by Albert and Allen Hughes
Starring Johnny Depp and Heather Graham

Like many young black filmmakers who bum-rushed the film scene in the 90s, the Hughes brothers' film school was also the world of rap music videos. Twin brothers Albert and Allen cut their cinematic teeth by directing a slew of West Coast gangsta rap videos when that genre was just beginning to make noise. They followed up their foray into music videos with their gritty debut feature *Menace II Society* and the rest was history. *Menace* became a cult hit, the brothers became players in Hollywood, and they followed up with Dead

Presidents, a critical, if not box office, hit. Then they went Hollywood to play with the big boys, to try and make a blockbuster. Did they succeed? Well, *From Hell* looks damn good, Johnny Depp turns in a twisted and watchable performance, and the production design is on point. But in between all of that there is a certain vacuousness about the film. As a matter of fact, one could say it is kind of soulless.

The title of the film comes from what Jack the Ripper was purported to have signed his letters with — his address, so to speak. And the London in the movie most certainly resembles Hell. The time is 1888 and mutilated bodies of prostitutes start turning up. Johnny Depp steps onscreen as the opium-puffing, clairvoyant Inspector Aberline of Scotland Yard to save the day.

With brilliant detective work and an all-seeing mind's eye, our hero Aberline traces the trail of blood from the gutters of the slums of London to the gilded halls of Buckingham Palace and finally to the spiritual apex of high society: the secret society of the Masons.

The tension from the plot comes mostly from the fact that Aberline has fallen in love with one of the intended victims (played by Heather Graham) so he's in a race against time to stop the killer before he gets to her.

The twists and turns in *From Hell* are exciting enough, and the world of nineteenth century London feels real enough, but at its heart the film is ultimately just a typical paint-by-numbers thriller, on par with a good episode of *Hill Street Blues*. It's all pacing and no pay-off. And for a film that promises density, it comes off as flat. It isn't surprising to learn that the script was adapted from a comic book. It shows.

So here we are years later and the Hughes brothers, those fresh, fierce voices of the new black cinema, have returned. Only it's not black cinema this time, no, this time it is pure Hollywood: big budget, an A-list actor and a Tinseltown it-girl. Seems that the one-time gangsta rap videomeisters wanted to come big this time. Good for them.

***

He Got Game

Written & directed by Spike Lee
Starring Denzel Washington and Ray Allen

The really good things about Spike Lee's newest film *He Got Game* are Denzel Washington and the title song by Public Enemy. The bad thing about Spike's new joint is everything else. The premise is juicy: a black father is offered early parole from the state pen by the governor of the state if the he convinces his estranged son to attend the governor's alma mater, Big State.

It's a seemingly perfect set up for Spike Lee, the revolutionary with a camera, to indict big time American college basketball for all its inequities and hypocrisy. Thrown into the mix is the spectre of Denzel's accidental murder of his wife, his son's mother. Two great story lines with which to build a moving and powerful film, right? Wrong. Nothing doing. All Spike does is serve up visual clichés of salivating coaches and agents going through the motions in their hunger for black athletic talent. You can get more insight into that world in your average sports page than what you're privy to in this film. There is hardly anything new here.

Jesus Shuttlesworth is the number one ranked high school basketball player in America. He has one week to decide which school he will attend on a full athletic scholarship. In that week, he will be re-united with his father, betrayed by (his) love, fucked by white women courtesy of one university, and courted by the NBA. Jake Shuttlesworth, locked up in prison for killing his wife, has one week to convince his son Jesus to attend Big State university so that rabid b-ball fan the state governor will be happy and set him free. The only problem is that Jesus hates his father. So begins our tale.

All we can do is hope that Spike does his duty in the main subplot involving the father-son relationship between Denzel and basketball wunderkid Ray Allen of the Milwaukee Bucks. The story about a father and a son feeling their way to reconciliation after dad killed mom, albeit accidentally, could be a really interesting, involving tale. This could be enough to carry a whole film if done well, right? Wrong. Spike strikes out big time here as well. Such a delicate subject would be a test for the best-trained actor to bring off, so what can you expect from a well-trained basketball player in this position, with this part? Not much. Ray Allen playing the estranged son to Denzel's apologetic father can be charming and not that bad at times, but should we pay eight bucks for not bad? I don't think so.

It makes you wonder what Spike was thinking in casting a non-trained actor to try and hold his own opposite the likes of an actor of Denzel's calibre in such a sublime performance. As an actor, Ray Allen makes a pretty good ball player, but unfortunately, it's not vice-versa.

Surely the most absurd and weakest aspect of the film is the plotline concerning Denzel and an abused young white hooker played by Milla Jovovich. Considering that Denzel has made a point of not making love to white women onscreen, you'd think he would wait for that special film in which to cross the color line and lose his "virginity."

As the film unfolds we learn more of the history of the father-son relationship that the film purports to be about, but not enough to save the film. Father pushed son too hard to excel? Been there, done that. Black man is imprisoned although he is essentially innocent? Been there, seen that. White America is out to exploit black talent. Hmmm.... Tried-and-true stuff, huh? The whole film seems to be constructed of American film truisms but not in a particularly interesting manner, the way that Tarantino does it. But as always, this Spike Lee joint looks amazing and the editing and camera work is quite innovative. Then again, so is every two-bit music video these days.

The truly sad thing about *He Got Game* is that its structural shortcomings only serve to illustrate what a fantastic actor Denzel Washington is. But here it is as if he is in a whole other film, a good film. If only Denzel's performance could be surgically removed and grafted onto a story worth his effort and our interest.

Spike is a well-known fixture at Madison Square Gardens where he is always on hand to cheer on his beloved New York Knickerbockers. And Spike is somewhat of a historian of basketball, having penned a book of musings on his relationship to the game last year, so you would think that with this sense of intimacy and his keen social eye, he could come up with something better than a more expensive version of the hood flick *Above the Rim*.

***

I Spy

Directed by Betty Thomas
Starring Eddie Murpy and Owen Wilson

Eddie's funnier than ever in this loose remake of the groundbreaking series *I Spy*. Though Eddie Murphy didn't invent the black guy/white guy buddy flick, he did perfect it in the 80s. Eddie Murphy films like *Beverly Hill's Cop*, *Trading Places*, and *48 Hours* struck box office gold time after time by partnering America's hottest black comic and a white star (Ackroyd, Nolte).

And though this formula wasn't fool-proof for Eddie, as we saw in his abysmal movie *Metro*, Hollywood decided to give it another try, and it works. Eddie is the funniest he's been in years.

In the 60s, Bill Cosby and Robert Culp starred in *I Spy*, the first interracial drama on network TV. The show — a funky spy series that had our two heroes globetrotting and saving the world all while posing as a tennis pro and trainer (Cosby played the trainer) — was a big hit with audiences and showed that America was ready to embrace a black TV hero.

In this film, the tennis pro has been changed to a champion boxer, and the black/white roles are reversed — Eddie plays the athlete, boxer Kelly Robinson, and Owen Wilson plays the trainer/agent Alex. The plot in this big budget remake is simple: the Switchblade, the most sophisticated prototype stealth fighter created yet, is stolen from the U.S. government, and it's up to Alex and Kelly to bring it back. Alex is a top spy and is reluctantly teamed up with the cocky civilian fighter to save the day. Though the premise is pretty standard, the interplay between the all too earnest Owen Wilson and Eddie's maniacal boxer is what makes this movie a hit. Like *The Nutty Professor* and *Doctor Dolittle*, Eddie does a great job in recreating classic characters with his wicked brand of humour. You gotta see it.

***

Lethal Weapon 4

Directed by Richard Donner
Starring Mel Gibson, Danny Glover, Joe Pesci, Rene Russo, Chris Rock, Jet Li

The numeral "four" in the title says it all. What film with the number four at the end of the title was ever any good? Even Cubby Broccoli had the sense to give all the James Bond films a separate new title. And it's *Henry V*, not *Henry IV*, that Branagh did. The catchphrase of the film is, "I'm too old for this shit," and "shit" is the key word with regards to this film.

This typical Hollywood story-by-committee has Riggs (Gibson) and Murtaugh (Glover) tackling middle age. Murtaugh is about to be a granddad and Peter Pan-ish Riggs is about to be a daddy. Add to the mix an Asian slave-labour smuggling ring and some cockamamie thematic connection between slavery's Middle Passage that Murtaugh goofily feels and off we go... When the original *Lethal Weapon* came out in '87, the mixture of Gibson's psycho cop with a death wish and Glover's middle class officer waiting for retirement was both funny and edgy. Fans couldn't help but root for these two.

However for this installment (and the last one for that matter), Richard Donner forgoes character development and instead goes for more slam-bams.

Along for the ride for comic relief is usual suspect Joe Pesci with his irritating trademark utterance, "Okay, okay, okay," and he's funny for about a minute, especially when seen next to the crackle of Chris Rock's Sergeant Butters. Lotsa explosions, unfunny lines, and a bunch of tried-and-true fight scenes makes *Lethal Weapon 4* a bad movie, just one of the many thunderous summer collages to munch popcorn by. And if you've seen one, you've seen them all. Yawn.

***

Money Train

Directed by Joseph Ruben
Starring Wesley Snipes and Woody Harrelson

Renegade transit cops fed up with the system plan to heist the train that transports all the subway cash — sound thrilling? It's not. Woody Harrelson and Wesley Snipes goof about in ninety minutes worth of disjointed scenes often peppered with gratuitous violence.

The chemistry that sparked between these two in *White Men Can't Jump* does not make an appearance in *Money Train* at all. The running gag that the two are foster brothers is weak. No real emotion seems to exist between the two, which is one of the key ingredients needed for this story to work.

The only thing to look forward to therefore is the heist. After a few paper-thin attempts at character motive, the script finally introduces the heist in the waning minutes of the film.

Without any definitive bad guys to root against or any likeable good guys to care about, the film just seems to go nowhere and do nothing. Skip it.

***

Unbreakable

Directed by M. Night Shyamalan
Starring Bruce Willis and Samuel L. Jackson

At some point during the second hour of *Unbreakable* I got "out of the moment" and realized there's not much going on here. That's a bad sign for a movie.

But it's not a bad movie. In fact it's a good film. But therein lies the dichotomy of *Unbreakable*. It's a good film but not a great movie. Meaning, it tells a story in a unique way, but it doesn't blow you away, the way most big budget movies should.

What's *Unbreakable* about? It's hard to say. It's like a trick photograph that looks like something different from whatever angle you look at it from. On a basic level, *Unbreakable* is a thriller. But just as Shyamalan's first film,

The Sixth Sense was a love story masquerading as a horror film and vice versa, so, too, is *Unbreakable*. It is a love story masquerading as an existential thriller about man's search for himself. And as is becoming this director's signature climax, it has an ending with a twist.

Unbreakable follows midlife David Dunn, played by Shyamalan's favourite star, Bruce Willis. Dunn is an ex All-American college football player whose inevitable pro career was quashed due to a car accident injury. Since then Dunn has lived an extremely average life, marrying his high school sweetheart, and working a monotonous job as a security guard at the university football stadium where he was once a star. But when Dunn survives a catastrophic train wreck — in fact, as the sole survivor — things start to change.

Elijah Price, an eccentric comic book collector played delightfully weird by Samuel L. Jackson, contacts Dunn. Where Dunn is seemingly unbreakable, Price is extremely breakable due to a rare brittle bone disease. Price slowly convinces Dunn that he is a real life superhero, so much so that Dunn, in the climax of the movie, saves the day the way a superhero should: defeating a super-villain in a violent clash.

But this being an existential thriller, the true identities of our characters are revealed at the very end, and it's not what you think. There are so many layers to *Unbreakable* that it is hard to gauge exactly what the film is trying to say. The overriding theme is superheroes and comic books and what exactly is a superhero.

But just as all the dead bodies and gore in *The Sixth Sense* served only to underscore the fact that it was really a forgettable story about how much Bruce Willis loved his wife, *Unbreakable*, too, is finally a forgettable story about how much a man loves his wife.

That said, I found the reverential tone and poetic sombreness of the movie stuck in my psyche like a pleasant aftertaste. It had that effect throughout the night and started again when I woke up the next morning. In fact, I believe that the story and performances of *Unbreakable* have permanently attached themselves to my cerebral cortex. That is the power of this film.

***

Vampire in Brooklyn

Directed by Wes Craven
Starring Eddie Murphy

At the height of his comedic powers, Eddie Murphy was the only comedian who could sell out Madison Square Gardens. People wanted to watch him on stage and on film. Lately however, Murphy has become increasingly unwatchable. *Vampire in Brooklyn* is another vehicle that illustrates his staleness. Murphy plays a Caribbean vampire scouring Brooklyn in search of an ideal mate: a half-human half-vampire beauty played by Angela Bassett. Murphy is able to strike a suave pose as the debonair drakoola, but it is wooden at best. The one bright spot in this dismal exercise is when Eddie's vampire morphs himself into a preacher and convinces the congregation that "evil is good." It's an all-too-brief flicker of what used to make us want to watch him.

***

Wild Wild West

Directed by Barry Sonnenfeld
Starring Will Smith, Kevin Kline, Kenneth Branagh, Salma Hayek

Something bigger and subtextual is always happening when you watch a Will Smith blockbuster. It's kind of the same way as when Eddie Murphy plays a detective or a conman or a college professor — you're watching Eddie being Eddie and trying not to get caught up in all that messy story stuff.

Watching Will is a bit like that. It's like you're watching the African-American dream come to fruition. You can't help but like the fact that Will is conquering the box office with as little skill as a Bruce Willis or a Harrison Ford. Black mediocrity has arrived. With that said, *Wild Wild West* and its lack of depth and plot go a long way to prove that Will Smith has that undeniable quality that all megastars have: charm in front of the camera.

In every generation, black America produces another conglomerated star, someone who has built on the previous stars — Poitier built on Robeson, Murphy built on Pryor, Denzel built on Poitier. Will is a great postmodern, post-hip-hop hero, both in real life and onscreen. He has the great benefit of being able to borrow from a smorgasbord of influences, both real and fictional.

Like a masterful rap star who samples the old funk of James Brown, the new funk of Parliament, and the present day stories of ghetto culture to form hip-hop, so, too, is Will Smith able to take a bit from Poitier, a bit from Malcolm X, a bit from Run-DMC, a bit from Sesame Street, a bit from I Dream of Jeanie, and blend it all into a potent postmodern, post-hip-hop, all-charming riff.

It's no surprise that with this cultural arsenal at his disposal, Will Smith is able to plug into a mediocre sitcom from the sixties and infuse it with enough sound and fury that it actually comes off as a great popcorn movie, despite all the things it has going against it.

The story remains fairly faithful to its impetus from the 60s as it follows superstud agent Jim West (Will Smith) and his absent-minded gadget man Artemis Gordon (Kevin Kline) as they do battle against evil in the old West. For this film, evil is deliciously played by Kenneth Branagh as the antebellum scientist Loveless. To their credit, the filmmakers put in several clever black references to the fact that our hero in 1860s America is a newly freed black man.

Critics have said that *Wild Wild West* will be second only to *Star Wars* at the box office this summer. That's cool because it means it will be another chapter in Will Smith's epic life.

Big, Bad (as in 'Awful') Black Movies

Half Past Dead

Written and directed by Don Michael Paul
Starring Steven Seagal and Ja Rule

The great actor Samuel L. Jackson said recently that rappers in movies is a bad thing; Ja Rule's performance in this action thriller is an example of what he meant. That's not to say that the star, Steven Seagal, is any great shakes because he's no better. But if you like Morris Chestnut a lot then go see *Half Past Dead*. 'Cause he's the only good thing in this weak rip off of the movie *The Rock*. Otherwise, stay away. It's pretty bad.

Chestnut plays criminal mastermind Donny/49er #1 who has infiltrated a high tech prison in order to force a death row inmate to give up the whereabouts of $200 million worth of gold that he's hidden in there. Unfortunately, undercover FBI agent Sascha (Steven Seagal) is in deep cover as a fellow inmate and he's out to stop him.

The title "*Half Past Dead*," comes from the fact that in the opening minutes of the film Seagal is shot up in a blazing gun battle and his heart actually stops for 22 minutes, leaving him half past dead — get it? The twist in the film is that rather than it being a prison movie about criminals trying to break out — it's about criminals trying to break in. Not to mention the fact that this isn't your run of the mill prison, this is the state of the art prison — the new Alcatraz.

The "new Alcatraz" is about to have its first execution when the party is spoilt by 10 commandos led by Morris Chestnut who parachute onto the island in the midst of a violent rain storm and take everyone hostage, including some high ranking government officials who were on hand to witness the execution.

But as in most of Seagal's films, the bad guys hadn't counted on some one on the inside being a trained killer. From that point it's pretty standard Seagal fare with him kicking everybody's butt. Nothing new.

***

Formula 51

Directed by Ronny Yu
Starring Samuel L. Jackson and Robert Carlyle

Formula 51 is not necessarily a bad movie, it's just an incoherent movie, which is usually worse. Samuel L. Jackson stars in this dopey would-be actioncomedy.

The film opens with Elmo double-crossing a would-be creepy kingpin played badly by Meatloaf. Elmo then hightails it to England with what everyone thinks is the formula to a funky new drug that is set to take the world by storm.

After an unwarranted violent opening, the film decides to become a comedy whenwe follow Elmo to the UK. Here *Formula 51* tries to do an imitation of *Snatch* and *Lock, Stock & 2 Smoking Barrels*. But whereas those films are slick and funny, this one is just slow and bizarre.

Elmo's plan in England is to try and set up the "big deal" for his new designer drug. The plan goes all-wrong in a way that's supposedly comical but is not really. Elmo winds up stuck in Liverpool with a reluctant escort, a low-level baddie played by Robert Carlyle. So while Elmo just wants to sell his stuff and jet, and Carlye just wants tickets to the Liverpool soccer game, they instead become entangled in a stupid web of double-dealing and double-crosses. The film also gives us one of the least sexiest sex scenes in which Carlyle and the hit woman who's on Elmos's tail do it in the tub of his mom's grimy bathroom.

The director Ronny Yu made some of the sequels to the Chucky movies (*Bride of Chucky*, etc.) which are bad movies in a funny way. This film is just strange and weird in very unfunny ways. Although I should say that Robert Carlye is truly a charismatic actor — he was really fun to watch and listen to. This movie is a waste of time. Skip it.

***

Out of Sync

Directed by Debbie Allen
Starring LL Cool J

LL Cool J is LA's "coolest" DJ, the Saint, in this badly acted, badly scripted, badly photographed movie. The non-existent plot gets underway when the Saint, who owes his bookie thirty grand falls into a (yawn) web of underworld murder and mayhem.

Sitcom veterans, Debbie Allen (*A Different World*) directed and Tim Reid (*WKRP in Cincinnati*) produced *Out-of-Sync* with all their sitcom values well intact. The film is an apparent attempt to tap into the lucrative urban black movie-going audience, with laughable chances of a theatrical release (thus the swift path to the video shelf).

Often, even in the lamest of movies there is some spark, something to ease the tedium, either the music or some unknown actor running around nabbing scenes, but *Out-of-Sync* has nothing, nothing at all. Ugh!

***

White Man's Burden

Directed by Desmond Nakano
Starring John Travolta, Harry Belafonte

In this directorial debut director/screenwriter Desmond Nakano said that he wanted to make a film with a "unique and provocative view on race." The film is neither provocative nor unique. It is slow and obscure.

Nakano is a Japanese-American screenwriter known for such scripting credits as *Last Exit to Brooklyn* and *American Me*, both critical, if not commercial, successes that illustrated powerful tales of struggling individualism amidst suffocating con-

formity. In *American Me*, the claustrophobic context was a violent prison in California, and in *Last Exit*, it was a seemingly inescapable social and physical ghetto. In *White Man's Burden*, Nakano sets the action (and I use the term loosely) in motion within a fictional alter-universe/city where blacks are the ruling elite of business and glamour and whites are mere peon ghetto dwellers.

Anti-hero Louis Pinnock, played adequately by now-hot John Travolta, is mistakenly fired due to an unintentional indiscretion while making a delivery to a powerful businessman's mansion. The businessman in question is Thaddeus Thomas, played by the ever-wooden Harry Belafonte. Belafonte rasps his way through WMB as a fundamental industrialist who is kidnapped by a distraught Pinnock and, like the movie's audience, is forced to roam endlessly without any real purpose. Pinnock is distraught after he loses his job and thus his home and family due (indirectly) to an off-the-cuff remark made by Thaddeus Thomas.

WMB seeks to tear away a familiar social and economic contextual skin and then "flip the script" in order to show the cruelty and absurdity that the politics of race in America creates in its people. Instead of wowing the audience with any astounding revelations, the film simply succeeds in offending us all, across the board. The black viewer has to sit there and view purported white-skinned versions of themselves acting ill-speaking (Travolta jives up his entire dialogue), violent (the white ghetto dwellers attack a pair of police officers in their attempt to subdue Pinnock, thus insinuating that all the rage that some segments of black society feel toward law enforcement is simply reactionary at best), and libidinous (Pinnock ogles Thomas' beautiful black wife and thus sees his already precarious life unravel). While WMB is kind enough to flesh out individualized insults of blacks and whites, it provides just one huge sweeping insult for every other ethnicity by simply excluding them. No Asians or Hispanics exist in this universe. In the politics of race in America, the black man is no longer the invisible man? It's anyone else who falls outside of the done-to-death black-white spectrum that isn't given visibility now. Though the exclusion is no doubt an exercise in artistic license to prove the proverbial point, America's media preoccupation with things only black and white succeeds in a maleficent negation of the rest of the world. Nakano populates the story with such "eye-opening" scenes as Pinnock's little white son coveting a black superhero doll over a white one.

That doesn't quite fit the role reversal theme because of the fact that Michael Jordan & Shaq loom larger than any Marvel or DC concoction could ever in the minds of young white America.

A few well-made points are driven home with sledgehammer self-aplomb (white homeless kids at the black fashion show), rather than a more effective subtle approach. After much meandering, the languid exercise culminates in a poor poetic attempt to jerk at some tears and an apparent attempt at showing that we "should all just get along." Despite a promising premise of scathing social commentary, WMB opts to insult and meander in lieu of any sort of focal point on which all the narrative points can converge.

***

UK Black

Babymother

Written & Directed by Julian Henriques
Starring Anjela Lauren Smith and Wil Johnson

In the mid-60s young Afro-American culture announced itself with the booming basslines and articulate rage of hip-hop music, and by the late 80s, young black filmmakers had visualized the hip-hop movement with films like *Menace II Society* and *Do The Right Thing*. Now in the late nineties the same thing is happening to Jamaican dancehall. Last year's film *Dance Hall Queen* and this year's *Babymother* are just two films that depict the ghetto glam of dancehall culture.

Babymother follows its heroine Nita as she struggles with motherhood and other pressures, all while trying to be heard by the world. Nita and her two girlfriends want in on the lucrative dancehall scenes as performers, but with her mother's death and her dancehall superstar boyfriend's indifference to her aspirations, Nita must navigate the streets and nightlife of black London to find a way to have her say on stage. The story is layered with twists and turns throughout, all of which subtly comment on what it means to be a black Briton in the present day.

As is expected, the music is top-notch and Angela Lauren Smith, who plays Nita, does a terrific job in capturing the chameleon-like quality that these black girls possess. She effortlessly transforms from stern mom to homegirl to sexually raunchy dancehall queen all in the blink of an eye. *Babymother* is a must see.

***

Sidney's Chair

Directed by Robert Bangura

Sometimes the beauty of films lie not in the lessons they teach, but rather in the subtle manner in which they illustrate a moment. Roberto Bangura's short *Sidney's Chair* uses the London suburb of Stepney as the backdrop and mechanism to give us a peek at a day in the life of your average biracial kid, Ricci.

The year is 1967, and to spice things up, Bangura has Sidney Poitier in the neighborhood shooting the classic *To Sir With Love*. The short plays out like a microcosm depicting the genesis of the multicultural society of London today.

Stepney, a dockyard community, is a typical gateway where the world makes its entrance onto the shores and eventually into the streets of London and eventually England. There's no political subtext here but rather an honest and beautifully looking recreation of childhood through the eyes of one of these new "toffee-colored" English kids.

The plot involves Ricci and his gal pal swiping Sidney Poitier's chair from the film set after being mistreated by some film set peon. The theft gives us the opportunity to observe the inner workings of Ricci's family, at the centre of which is the strained relationship between Ricci and his dark-skinned African father.

The filmmaker throws into the midst of this typical father-son antagonism the fact that Ricci harbors ill feelings towards his father's color and thus his own color. He even goes so far as to ask his mum who is the lighter out of he and his sister. It speaks softly yet clearly about the low racial esteem that these children of color often must deal with from a young age. We witness several more scenes, such as Ricci's father defending his son against an angry bigot, a touching scene of maternal comfort, and finally Ricci returning the chair and getting Sidney's autograph.

Aside from a harmless black vagrant who wan-ders throughout a few scenes and whose role doesn't seem to be really defined, there is a sense of completeness by the time the film ends. Overall, though, it seems to lack a focal point at which the narrative is drawn to. *Sidney's Chair* doesn't linger long after the lights go up, but it does work in its own muddled and harmless way.

***

Soul Survivors

Directed by Sandy Johnson
Starring Ian McShane

At its heart, *Soul Survivors* is a heartwarming, funny story about a dreamer on an odyssey to find that which once made him happy. Unfortunately, in its execution *Soul Survivors* is a sappy, predictable baby-boomer piece of nostalgic fluff. The truly sad thing about the film is that the creative team behind it is the same team behind the brilliant BBC series LOVEJOY: Ian McShane and Martyn Auty.

The film follows the quest of Otis Cooke, played by Ian McShane, an English radio DJ who lives too vicariously through the sixties soul music of his radio program. When the station fires him in the name of automation, Otis suddenly has nothing to live for. As is the norm for these sort of quixotic tales, Otis sets off to recapture his "soul."

In Otis' case, it's a soul song by the long forgotten soul group The Tallahasses. Otis worships the group's old hit "Pickin' Up the Pieces" and is convinced that if he can just get to America, track down the guys, reunite them, and bring them back to the UK to perform, than all will be right in the world. Needless to say, Otis succeeds in this task, but not without the required generic plot twists involving shady lawyers and hookers with hearts of gold. Back in the UK, the ho-hum concert is a hit, the band is a hit again, and as the corny titles tell us in the end, everyone lives happily ever after.

The one saving grace of *Soul Survivors* is the soundtrack that contains all the hits from that era, but even that doesn't make up for the film's extreme lack of humour and drama. There's also the sick irony of seeing blaxploitation stalwarts Antonio Fargas and Isaac Hayes play nothing but living toys for the wacky Englishman to relive his youth. Shaft wouldn't have went out that way.

Southern Discomfort

Eve's Bayou

Written and Directed by Kasi Lemmons
Starring Samuel L. Jackson and Debbi Morhan

"Memory is a selection of images. Some elusive, others printed indelibly on the brain...."
—Eve Batiste

Gumbo is a southern dish that probably grew out of necessity rather than any serious culinary adventure. It consists of potatoes, shrimp, beef, pork, carrots, and more, plus the kitchen sink. Simply put, gumbo is made from what you got, and because of that, the dish is both simple and complex at the same time.

Eve's Bayou, by first time director Kasi Lemmons, is sort of the cinematic equivalent of a gumbo – simple and complex. Like gumbo, it involves a multitude of ingredients: Dr. Batiste is the philandering "best black doctor" in town, his beautiful wife suffers quietly and his two daughters fight for his attention. The doctor's sister, Aunt Mozzelle, is the local clairvoyant whose husbands all meet with untimely deaths. The real dilemma arises when, in a whisky soaked haze, the doctor breaks a sacred taboo — or does he? In this racial potpourri that exists on the moss-draped, foggy banks of a swamp known as *Eve's Bayou*, nothing is what it seems.

The heart of *Eve's Bayou* is a simple and poetic tale of betrayal. Like a spoonful of gumbo, it quickly becomes something else. It becomes a story of revenge, a story of womanhood, a story of lust, a story based on a memory that may or may not be correct.

Using the point of view of ten-year old Eve Batiste, Lemmons spins a yarn that treads deliciously between fact and fantasy, legend and reality. Even the all-black setting of the bayou with its French speaking Negroes, country doctors, and haute-coutured women seems to be pure fiction steeped in a historical reality.

The bayou of the title was apparently given to a beautiful African slave by a grateful French gentleman whom this woman saved from death with the aid of ancient and spiritual charms. In return, the Frenchman gave the woman her freedom, the bayou, and lastly, a multitude of children. Eve is one of her descendants.

Eve is the precocious youngest daughter who constantly seems to lose out to her older sister for the affections of her father, a suave country doctor played by Samuel L. Jackson. As Eve stumbles towards womanhood behind her increasingly elegant sister, they both come to realize that the innocent flirtatious charms that their father offers his adoring women patients are not that innocent. During one moist and simmering summer, as his wife, lovers, and two daughters achingly and ferociously seek out his acceptance, the "good" country doctor implodes with the aid of a jealous husband.

Like a Tennessee Williams play, *Eve's Bayou* is a story steeped in the traditional southern gothic. It's about mixed blood and sexuality and how these internal warring factions come to a head on hot summer nights. It is simple and complex.

***

A Lesson Before Dying

Directed by Joseph Sargant
Starring Don Cheadle and Mekhi Phifer

A Lesson Before Dying is a touching tale about dignity — the much-needed, often elusive, dignity for blacks in the South in the forties. Novelist Ernest J. Gaines revisits the themes of family ties, dignity and hope that he explored in his classic novel *The Autobiography of Miss Jane Pittman*. The film boasts an extremely competent cast including

Cicely Tyson, Mekhi Phifer, and Don Cheadle among others.

Cheadle plays the lead, Grant Wiggins, an educated black man who chooses to teach the black children at the small, ill-equipped schoolhouse on the plantation rather than at the "shiny new" school in town. He is a man of conviction and also a man of sorrow. Despite his intellect, he sees daily how the sweltering racism in his home of rural Louisiana douses the dreams and hopes of the children that he teaches year after year. Wiggins is like Sisyphus, forever fighting a losing, uphill battle. So it's no wonder that Wiggins is skeptical and reluctant to "tutor" a deathrow inmate in the weeks leading up to his execution. The inmate is played with a beautiful, simmering quality by Mekhi Phifer (*Clockers*). Phifer is wrongly convicted of killing a white man and is sentenced to death. But the spectre of death is not the real tragedy in this young man's ordeal; the real tragedy is that his incompetent and racist defense lawyer had argued in court for his innocence on the grounds that he is nothing but a "stupid hog." The shame felt by Phifer's grandmother in the courtroom that day is pure psychic pain that has been built up over centuries of slavery and bigotry. The grandmother has it in her mind that her boy will not go to his death believing that he is as worthless as a hog, so Wiggins is co-opted into meeting with Phifer in jail daily to rebuild his dignity so that he may walk to the gallows a man.

What comes from having these two vastly different black men in the South thrown together is a beautiful and touching story of friendship and male bonding. The film may not pack the cinematic and narrative punch that *The Autobiography of Miss Jane Pittman* did, but the performances are solid and the story compelling. It's good storytelling.

***

Once Upon A Time... When We Were Colored

Directed by Tim Reid
Starring Al Freeman Jr.

Tim Reid's directorial debut *Once Upon A Time... When We Were Colored* is a well-crafted piece of American nostalgia and history based on Clifton Taubert's acclaimed book of the same name.

It is a beautifully-lensed film which revels in all the different hues of brown skin, constructs a poignant coming-of-age story, and uses the protagonist's eyes to vigorously show the dichotomatic cruelty and sweetness of growing up black in

America in a telling matter-of-fact tone. Such a bittersweet blend is best illustrated when Cliff, the young narrator, is berated by his white employer for being too lazy to read because, as she says, "There are more than enough books at the public library for a hungry mind."

Cliff offers quite plainly in return, "Coloreds aren't allowed in the library, Miss." Reid populates this film with an array of familiar faces: everyone from Shaft himself to Mrs. Huxtable struts their stuff before the camera, invoking a chemistry that beams off of the screen. The filmmakers have been practical enough to infuse several points of dramatic tension with down-home jukebox-joint brawls and menacing KKK posturing to keep the treacly nostalgic story honest. The power of the film culminates as the narrator, now grown, heads north by train, and a montage of all of the love and guidance that the black and sometimes white townspeople have had to offer him whips by on the screen, jerking at his tears and ours.

Like a painting, the film *Once Upon A Time... When We Were Colored* starts out with very tiny strokes that don't seem like much and then adds a few more.

Varying colors are added, splashed, and smeared onto the canvas. A certain tempo is detected in the matching and blending of colors and forms. A definitive voice gradually becomes discernible as the once tiny piece grows and grows. Some strokes of the brush are done with an urgency and deliberateness while others are done with the nonchalance of an afterthought.

Back and forth this process continues, and your eyes snatch up chunks of it as they're incorporated into the rest of the components on the canvas.

It's a bit confusing at times, but then comes the payoff. Several gentle strokes complete the collage, and the beauty and force of the work begins to pour off of the canvas as one. It brings tears to your eyes because you not only understand it, but you've watched it grow and bloom, and that in itself is part of its beauty.

***

Remember the Titans

Dir. By Boaz Yakin
Starring Denzel Washington

I love football and I love football movies. And I have a theory: Football movies can't lose with North American audiences. Sure you have some exceptions like *Little Giants* but for the most part, football on the big screen rocks!

Even a paint by numbers picture like *The*

Replacements starring Keanu Reeves (as a quarter-back!) found an audience. And the list goes on: *Varsity Blues, Any Given Sunday* — and how else can you explain the huge success of a piece of sh#t like Adam Sandler's *The Waterboy*? It's football. That's how.

This brings us to *Remember the Titans*, the latest film from the writer/director of the critically acclaimed film, *FRESH*. Titans is based on a true story about the racial integration of a small high school in Virginia in 1971. The pain and the glory of this social experiment is seen through the eyes of the football team, the Titans. Up until 1970 the team has been all white, but this year things are going to change. The white players are gonna have to compete for their positions against hungry black players.

Even worse, the school is forced to give the head coaching job to a black coach. This being the south, the white folks don't take to kindly to the idea. But this being a Disney film the racial violence is held to a minimum. And it's fun to watch how a movie about racial unrest in the south gets through the whole story without anyone uttering the word "nigger". It,s actually quite funny the euphemisms that constantly pop up in place of the infamous n-word.

The black coach is played by Denzel Washington with his usual excellence and Will Patton weighs in with an understated eloquence as the replaced white coach who has to swallow his pride and become a mere assistant under the new black coach.

With this premise in place, the film pretty much follows the standard M.O. of your typical "can't we all just get along" movie of the week on race relations. The black and white players at first hate each other but learn to understand, the respect and then even love each other. Eventually the love in spreads to the bigotted town folks and in the end like every good football movie, our team wins at the very last minute.

Sure the movie is full of sports clichés and race relation clichés and we don't really get any real insight into the great social experiment of forced integration but watching Denzel and Will Patton go through their paces and make some cheesy scenes and tired lines bring you to tears and make you cheer as they literally will this run of the mill script into a truly enjoyable movie.

Cause football movies can't fail. Just a theory.

Lone Wolves

DRUMLINE

Starring Nick Cannon
Directed by Charles Stone III

I loved *Drumline*. I mean I really loved it. Despite it's cheesy premise and pedestrian plot structure, I left the cinema felling exhilarated. The friend who saw the movie with me went as far as to corner the studio rep and proclaim his love of the film as well.

Now maybe it's cause I went to a black university in the south which is the world that *Drumline* is set, but I set aside my better judgment and overlooked all of the flaws of the movie and simply put, let myself be blown away. The film is set in the hyped and (believe it or not) high-stakes world of marching bands. The half-time marching bands that are the pride and joy of HBCU's in the states (Historically Black Colleges and Universities). As a matter of fact more fans come to check out the bands do their thing rather than the football game itself.

And for anyone unfamiliar with this unique brand of musical drama, the movie *Drumline* will serve it up in chunky portions. Like most movies that revolve around an exciting sub-culture, the plot is just a side dish to the main course — the performances — the drumline routines are what this movie is all about. And if you can stop yourself from laughing at the ridiculous band uniforms you'll get right into it.

Drumline stars popular Nickelodeon personality, Nick Cannon in what is essentially is a fish-out-of-water comedy. Nick plays Devon, a talented street drummer from Harlem who rolls up at Atlanta A & T to show the world what's up.

But Devon soon realizes that at this prestigious Southern University it'll take more than talent to reach the top and lead the drumline. And though Nick brings his Harlem world swagger down south beneath the Mason-Dixon line with him, his performance never sinks to caricature. And the film is also a welcome departure from the two types of black films that Hollywood seems to be making over and over — buppy bougeouise comedies and neo-coonish buddy flicks.

A famous football coach once said, to win a football game, you need three great plays and no bad ones. Similarly, a famous film director from Hollywood's golden era once said that to make a good movie, you need three great scenes and no bad ones. And the director seems to know this. He lets *Drumline* succeed on such a theory.

Though the director, Charles Stone II is best

known for creating and directing the hugely successful 'Whattssuupp! Budweiser commercials, he does an excellent job of raising the material above the plot and performances, which are fairly standard. His treatment of the band performance scenes are explosively good and Stone knows that Nick Cannon the lead has charisma to spare and he gives him the space to let it shine — so with those two things going for it, *Drumline* kicks ass and makes for a good movie.

***

Always Outnumbered

Directed by Michael Apted
Starring Laurence Fishburne

In between the supa-dupa-fly images of black culture that music videos promote and the larger-than-life superhero athletes who fly across football fields and basketball courts are the simple smaller-than-life stories. For an audience weaned on the amped-up view of what it means to be black, these gentle stories seem oddly out of place. But if these tales are given a chance, there's usually something just as important and just as powerful that's said.

Such is the case of the TMN cable movie *Always Outnumbered*.

Always Outnumbered is based on Walter Mosley's novel *Always Outnumbered, Always Outgunned*, and the title aptly describes the stress that the film's protagonist feels as he makes his way through the down-and-out streets of South Central Los Angeles. The guns referred to by the title are not the steels and gats and teks that rappers rage about, but instead the more powerful social weapons of mass destruction like poverty and unemployment.

Mosley is best known for his funky series of private eye novels featuring the heroic black private eye Easy Rawlins. A few years ago one of his novels was bought to the screen with Denzel Washington as Easy Rawlins in *Devil in a Blue Dress*. *Always Outnumbered* is definitely a detour from his usual pulp fiction genre style. The film presents Socrates Fortlow, an ex-con with a violent past, who moves to the sunny West Coast to start a new life. Instead all he finds are hard times.

Laurence Fishburne plays Socrates with his usual simmering concentration in this urban tale of an everyman trying to create some sort of meaning in his life as he struggles to make a living by collecting cans and looking for work. Michael Apted, the director behind *Gorillas in the Mist* and *Thunderheart* amongst others, is as well known for his documentary work (35 Up, 42) as for his theatrical works, and he does a capable and slow-moving job of spinning Socrates' quixotic fable in the urban jungles of LA.

Apted replaces warm sunshine, beaches, and palm trees for barred-up liquor stores that look like fortresses and homeless shantytowns. Like Don Quixote, Socrates has neither the means nor tools to save those in distress, yet he tries nonetheless. The structure of the story is episodic in the way that it presents Socrates with one victim after another. He is the first victim though — a victim of unemployment that he fights tooth and nail everyday.

Then there's Darryl, a 13-year-old modern day sepia orphan-Annie, who roams the streets without purpose until Socrates takes him under his wing. He teaches him to stand up to his outer demons (the neighborhood gang) and his inner demons (his guilt for having not helped a boy who was being stabbed to death). Socrates' next mission is to help mend the disintegration of a young couple who live on his street. The husband, played by Bill Nunn, is too proud to work at a menial job, and his family suffers for his pride. Socrates knocks some sense into him.

Finally, when his elderly best friend is diagnosed with fatal cancer and his Medicaid won't cover any treatment for the disease, it's up to 'Socco,' as he calls Fishburne's character, to procure some painkilling drugs in order to let his old friend leave this life in peace. All the tales are gradually weaved from beginning to end, occasionally stopping to make little bits of social commentary on how America treats its poor. And in the end, everything ends up nicely for everyone. One of the nicer things about *Always Outnumbered* is the way in which this inner city hero is allowed to solve his problems not just with violence but also with wisdom. Ultimately the film does a commendable job in giving voice to a black experience that too often is lost between the thunder of a slamdunk and the boom of a funky bass line.

***

Curtis's Charm

Directed by John L' Ecuyer
Starring Maurice Dean Wint, Callum Keith Rennie, Rachel Crawford

The low-tech, grit-and-grime look of Canadian indie *Curtis's Charm* definitely lends itself to this story, revolving 'round the voodoo-inspired delusions of a black junkie named Curtis. Local actor Maurice Dean Wint (*Rude, Tek Wars*) plays Curtis, a high-strung addict who's convinced that his mother-in-law is sabotaging his psyche with Haitian voodoo spells. While in the throes of this narco-spiritual dilemma, Curtis enlists the comfort of his friend from rehab, an ex-junkie named Jim who is played by Callum Keith Rennie (*Double Happiness*).

The two resemble overgrown kids playing truant from real life and responsibility as they bounce all over the city while Curtis retells his delusional tale in off-kilter flashbacks. The black-and-white film is the debut feature effort of John L'Ecuyer. The film is based on an eight-page story by junkie-turned-writer Jim Carroll (*The Basketball Diaries*).

L'Ecuyer first read the piece as an adolescent junkie himself. The filmmakers have done all that they can to parlay those eight pages into a feature length film, and you can definitely see the narrative stretching, almost tearing at its seams with its dia-logue-driven structure. It is punctuated all too often with ineffective dead spots, the characters just sit-ting around while the camera employs every zany angle to photograph these two against the tiresome grey background (and foreground, for that matter). In essence, what the film attempts to do is take the pitiful and sad subject of the jonez and withdrawal cycle, mix in a psycho-mental voodoo sub-theme, and then have the crazy, out-of-this world Curtis bounce off of Jim's stiff-as-board straight role in an attempt at dark humor. Dean Wint ticks and twitch-es all over the screen with bug-eyed aplomb, while Jim casually tags along and condescends to his friend with a narration that pops up now and again

as most of the jokes fall flat.

The structure is somewhat effective at blurring the lines between real and imagined when it comes to Curtis' paranoid psyche, and like Jim, we never know whether to believe this raving, hopped-up junkie or not. Wint's performance verges on being an outright hilarious endeavor, but never quite de-livers all of the goods because the gears and sprockets of his technique keep showing through, thus always letting us know that this is only a per-formance, a shtick. His tongue doesn't quite wrap around the dialogue before he spits out his words, so the lines come out sounding as if they are trapped in actor-trained vernacular and not from an over-the-edge crackpot. The film culminates when, in an effort to free Curtis from his demons, Jim fab-ricates a "charm" for Curtis to protect him from his mom-in-law's whammy. Curtis puts too much stock into this scrap of paper and in this state of per-ceived invulnerability is killed by another junkie whilst in search of the dopeman. Like most short stories there is no real dramatic arc guiding the characters, so the film simply ends without provid-ing any real answers or motives, such as why Curtis' wife even stays with his sorry ass. With limited re-sources and this sketchy genesis, *Curtis's Charm* makes the best of what it is: a pretty good short masquerading as a feature.

Antoine Fisher

Directed by Denzel Washington
Starring Denzel Washington and Derek Luke

One of the most hilarious novels I've ever read is *Home Repairs* by Trey Ellis. It is a fresh and funny coming-of-age story that unfolds in the form of a diary chronicling a young black man's zany ride into maturity through adventures and misadventures with the opposite sex, all while he tries to make it in the white man's world. Denzel Washington obviously felt the same way, because he snapped up the movie rights for his directorial debut and promptly had a script written by the author. I was excited. That was over a decade ago. Over ten years later, Denzel has chosen to make his directorial debut not with that comedic coming-of-age tale, but rather with a decidedly dramatic coming-of-age tale. The film *Antoine Fisher* is the poignant account of a young sailor (Derek Luke) with a violent and hair trigger temper. While in the navy, Antoine is sent to a naval psychiatrist (Washington) for help.

What follows is a cathartic releasing of pent up demons and emotions by Antoine, which in turn allows him to revisit his horrific childhood and to confront the painful past so that he may begin to heal. In this era of televised psychology by the likes of Oprah and Dr. Phil, a movie about coming to grips with the past doesn't exactly seem like what Hollywood would want to put up on the screen, but with an absolutely powerful script and Denzel's star power, this is an important movie to have in cinemas.

And though the strengths of this movie are the performances of Denzel and newcomer Derek Luke, the true star is the script as it adroitly captures that metaphysical chip that so many young black men carry on their shoulders and the strength that it takes to lift it off. Like the indie hit *Good Will Hunting*, *Antoine Fisher* also deals with the old psycho adage of broken children becoming broken adults. Antoine's backstory is an all-too-familiar one of neglect and abuse, and how even as adults those ghosts remain and cause the man to remain a broken boy inside. Denzel Washington as the Navy psychiatrist who is the key to Fisher's salvation turns in his usual riveting performance without stealing the show. It's a far cry from his Oscar winning turn as Alonzo, the immoral monster of narco agent in last year's Training Day.

Denzel is quoted as saying that his intention with the movie was to keep it simple and honest and forego the popular MTV style of directing that so often populates our movie screens today. It's about hearts and minds, he says, and that uncluttered earnest directing style allows what is a timeless story to unfold and come alive unencumbered.

***

Bamboozled

Written and Directed by Spike Lee
Starring Damon Wayans

The original revolutionary with a camera, Spike Lee, aims his celluloid bazooka at the TV world in his latest film, *Bamboozled*. The film features *In Living Color*'s Damon Wayans and *A Different World*'s Jada Pinkett-Smith. It is an attempt to be a daring and condemning satire of the inherent racism behind the scenes of American network television. Lee tries to be funny and insightful as he looks at how race and ratings cause an absurd pursuit to lead the ratings game in television. Unfortunately, he fails, but that's not to say that the film doesn't make you think at times. Damon Wayans, a brilliant comic mind, is one note and confusing as the star of the film. He plays uppity nigger Pierre Delacroix, a Harvard educated man who is the only black writer at upstart TV network Continental Network System. Pierre is desperate to get his very middle class show ideas to air. But his boss, excellently played by Michael Rapaport, is a wigger who proclaims to be blacker than Pierre, who therefore knows that 'niggers' don't wanna see that middle class bullshit. Feeling doomed, Pierre comes up with a brilliant stroke of subversive genius. He'll create the most racist show, get it on air, people will hate it, and thus prove that people don't real-

ly wanna see a modern 'coon' show. In fact he calls his 'monster' The New Millennium Minstrel Show. It's a variety show chock full of every ethnic stereotype from Aunt Jemima to Sambo. But in a sick and twisted turn of events, the show becomes a major hit, sponsored by a major malt liquour company. In the end, Pierre becomes seduced by his own show and actually begins to believe in it. It takes his young beautiful protégé Sloan Hopkins (Jada Pinkett-Smith) to put Pierre in check. But by then, it's too late. Spike's intentions are good, and he will definitely draw attention to a serious problem in American culture, but a better script coulda made this a classic in the vein of Network, which Spike Lee credits for being the inspiration for this film. Bright spots are Paul Mooney as Pierre's dad, a chitlin circuit comic, and Mos Def as a would-be five percenter. *Bamboozled* is a film to see for shock value, and it definitely shows that Spike is still not afraid to piss powerful people off. That's always good to see.

***

Bulworth

Directed by Warren Beatty
Starring Warren Beatty and Halle Berry

With Clinton's right-wing democratic politics making all the hopes of the yesteryear liberals seem like nothing but pipe dreams, the present state of these politics are causing said liberals to re-evaluate the situation. Warren Beatty, having earned his cinema-politic credentials with critically acclaimed *Reds*, weighs in again in the arena with the political comedy *Bulworth*. A glance at the list of artists on the *Bulworth* soundtrack lets you know right away that Beatty ain't aiming for the typical Hollywood whitewash of American politics. With Cappadonna, Ice Cube, and Ol' Dirty Bastard rippin' tha mic in the background, you know that Warren 'Shampoo' Beatty is tryin' somethin' different this time. First off, Beatty forgoes his typical leading lady for the delectable Halle Berry, who plays Nina, a politically conscious, ghetto-glam b-girl. And secondly, Beatty lets it all hang out, letting his character Senator Bulworth say and do everything and anything.

The premise offers up Senator Bulworth, a Democrat from California, as one of the white left wing liberals, à la Clinton, who went into government service to make a difference, and dare I say, change the world. But after years on Capitol Hill, the good senator has just become another piece of the problem: an official who represents big business rather than the little guy. The morally bankrupt senator does the only thing he can to wipe his slate clean: he orders a hit — on himself — while he swings through the last leg of his re-election campaign in LA. And from that point on, it's a nonstop trip that slices from mansions up in Beverly Hills down to the grim streets of South Central.

Not having slept or eaten in days and now having nothing to lose, Bulworth takes on all comers. When at a posh reception of leading Hollywood producers the senator muses belligerently on why Hollywood turns out such drivel if it is run by the best and brightest, it is as much a challenge as it is a condemnation. Then he takes on the insurance industry at a fundraiser at the Beverly Wiltshire. With mic in hand, Bulworth delivers a scathing and oft hilarious rap song that exposes the crookedness of corporate America's involvement in politics, much to the chagrin of his corporate supporters. It is not just white America that gets to feel the blast of truth from Bulworth's mic.

In full 'hood attire, Beatty disses and indicts those ghetto monsters who prey on their own kind in their lust for cash that they collect off of the misery of their brothers and sisters. Of course the film isn't just straight diatribe. Weaving in and out of the main plot are scenes involving his love interest Halle Berry, the impending hit, and a totally funny performance by Oliver Platt playing Bulworth's assistant. Amiri Baraka wanders through the story as a vagrant who repeats the line, "Be a spirit, not a ghost," like a mantra. At the beginning of *Bulworth* the senator sits in his posh Capitol Hill office dressed in typical government battle attire: blue suit, red tie, white shirt. At the end, Bulworth is sportin' Puma and Adidas and cruisin' the hood in a hooptey. He has indeed undergone the quintessential American the rags-to-riches trip.

All in all, *Bulworth* is really enjoyable entertainment. Beatty is as likeable as ever, the soundtrack is all that, and at times the script speaks truths which are often glossed over in such films. However, I would not to say that *Bulworth* is without fault. The structural jump that would have us believe that Bulworth wants to commit suicide is not clearly defined, and neither is the reason for why he changes his mind. The film also tends to be preachy at times, especially when it comes to dealing with the social ills affecting poor communities. And as much as Halle Berry is a treat to look at, she isn't all that believable as a girl from the 'hood. She simply came across as Halle Berry dressed up and tryin' to talk like she's from South Central.

In the end, as in most Hollywood morality tales, the eyes of the protagonist have been opened, and he has learned from his mistakes and will be a better man for it. With that the film is basically saying, 'Cut the shit, everybody!

Devil in a Blue Dress

Directed by Carl Franklin
Starring Denzel Washington and Jennifer Beals

Back in the funky seventies when Shaft was roaming the streets of Gotham and fighting crime, he probably wasn't too pressed about making his next mortgage payment. However, that is exactly what Easy Rawlins in 1948 Los Angeles is worried about — keeping his house beneath his feet, grounding himself in some semblance of the American Dream. Easy Rawlins is the sepia literary doppelganger to Raymond Chandler's Philip Marlowe. Created by black crime writer Walter Mosley, Easy is a black everyman set in morality tales where he seems to be the only one packing any morals at all. By combining Mosley's well-drawn characters and plots from his novel *Devil in a Blue Dress* with Denzel's charm and technique and an adequate budget from Tinseltown, director Carl Franklin has created a stylish noir. In the last act, Don Cheadle livens things up as trigger-happy Southerner named Mouse, a human pistol ever eager to go off.

***

Hav Plenty

Written, directed and starring Christopher Scott Cherot

Lee Plenty is my new anti-hero. Not since Wendell Harris smirked from the screen in *Chameleon Street* has a black movie character seemed so cool and detached, so complex and refreshing. Lee Plenty owes less to *Boyz N The Hood* and *Do The Right Thing*, and more to Nick Nolte's character "Jerry Baskin" in *Down and Out in Beverly Hills* and James Spader's character "Graham" in *Sex, Lies, and Videotape*. The story takes place over New Year's Eve weekend.

Upwardly mobile buppie Havilland Savage invites downwardly mobile slacker Lee Plenty to her mom's plush DC home to celebrate with her and her beautiful assured girlfriends out of pity. The sight of Lee with his unkempt hair and rumpled torn sweater amidst the sparkling polish of his bourgeoisie hosts sets the tone for Lee Plenty's psychosexual odyssey into the neurosis of these modern young women's sexuality. Like Whit Stilman's *Metropolitan*, these characters talk and talk and then talk some more, but the lines are crisp, the humour is dry, and the sexual tension mounts with every scene.

Writer/director Chris Scott Cherot knows his characters well and affectionately and is thus skillful enough to bring the latent sexual heat to a boil without even the slightest glimpse of flesh. He does this through innuendo, smirks, and luscious, lingering close-ups of lead actress Chenoa Maxwell. The only physically sexual act in the film is a kiss towards the end, but by that time the audience is so hot and bothered that the mere sight of this kiss is a great orgasmic release. Hill Harper, last seen in Spike Lee's *He Got Game*, weighs in as Havilland's sometime fiancé Michael Simmons. Harper has a lot of fun in the role as he tweaks the whole slick r&b bad-boy image that so often represents young black culture on BET. *Hav Plenty* offers a story and a hero that black audiences have been hungering for after a decade of two-dimensional black characters who were bustin' caps and mackin' honeys. Cherot offers us characters that revel in rhetoric and language. In the scene where usually the girl would find a gun or some other instrument of destruction and betrayal, Havilland Savage instead finds Lee's stethoscope and his copy of *Wuthering Heights*.

When this film was making the festival circuit it definitely was rough around the edges, but with Miramax picking it up for distribution and Babyface Edmonds (*Soul Food*) coming on as the executive producer, the influx of cash has definitely afforded Cherot the chance to clean up some technical glitches. Unfortunately, he has also taken away some of the charm. The ending, though meant to be tongue-in-cheek, comes across as just an afterthought happy ending.

67

This new ending lacks the poetic resonance of the original bittersweet ending. And considering that the film succeeds mostly because of its clever and insightful banter, some of the retorts from the original are sorely missed. In the original cut when Lee is asked why he broke up with his white girlfriend of five years, he replies, "Cause five years was long enough for a black man to go out with a white woman." Like the film itself, it doesn't seem like it makes sense, but it seems like it just might.

Panther

Directed by Mario Van Peebles
Starring Kadeem Hardison and Courtney B. Vance

The sophomore jinx seems to have carried over to his junior year for Mario Van Peebles. After stunning the industry by racking up over fifty million dollars with debut feature *New Jack City*, audiences were poised to gobble up Peebles' follow-up: A black western?! Hell yeah! But despite his good intentions and heart, *Posse* was a disappointment. Big Daddy Kane on horseback? I don't think so! Panther seems a sure fire hit in the midst of today's "black enlightenment" period, but no, it doesn't work. The funky camera style is still there, but it

ain't funky anymore — been there, seen that. And no matter how cool a cast you got, or how many nostalgic tunes you drape over it, the story has gotta grip you and coax you along. The historical significance of the Black Panthers is the stuff of which legends are made, but there are far too many narrative holes in this film that are covered by poor dramatic devices — fires, explosions, shootouts, and so forth — for it to work. With the dire straights that the black community finds itself in today, you, too, will want to find an emotional riveting story in *Panther*, but it ain't there.

***

Training Day

Directed by Antoine Fuqua
Starring Denzel Washington and Ethan Hawke

When Antoine Fuqua made his feature film debut with the under-whelming East-meets-West flick *The Replacement Killers*, it flopped at both the box office and with film critics across the continent. But for all of its shortcomings, *The Replacement Killers* had something going for it: style. The opening sequence of Chow Yun Fat mowing down a club full of Asian baddies is alone worth the price of admission. Fuqua, whose main calling card was the Coolio music video *Gangster's Paradise*, followed-up *Killers* with the Jamie Fox vehicle *Bait*. Though *Bait* came across as a poor man's *Enemy of the State*, it still worked on some level; it had a definite flair. Then came *Training Day*, and with an A-list star in Denzel and a budget big enough to be able to play with all the cinematic toys, Fuqua seemed poised to hit a home run after his first two strikes. Well, *Training Day* doesn't exactly leave the ballpark, but it's more than a single. Its success will depend on how much the audience is seduced by Denzel's sublime bad-guy turn. The movie's premise is as high concept as you can get — a rookie cop is given one day on the job to prove to the leader of an elite LAPD under-cover corps that he's got the skillz to make the team. Ethan Hawke, looking like an escapee from Starbucks, is the neophyte officer, while a macked-out and iced-out Denzel is the head officer in charge whom he has to impress. The plot isn't your typical Syd Field three-act offering. Instead, the plot more closely resembles one of the nihilistic rap songs that appear on the soundtrack for *Training Day*. Like one of these many gangsta rap homages to the eternal good vs. evil operas that play out in urban centres all over the world, so does the film riff rather than narratively illustrate. But at the end of the day all of that doesn't matter. What matters is that you totally get off on Denzel's incredible portrayal of a hood cop who's so deep, deep under-cover that he's drunk with the power that he pos-sesses in the underworld of pimps and hustlers, yet still is trying to please the pimps and hustlers at City Hall. Unfortunately, the ending descends into one of those typical drawn-out fight-to-the-last-drop sequences, but by that time you've been on such a roller coaster ride of ups and downs, twists and turns that you don't really care. Getting to watch good guy Denzel play a twisted HNIC (Head Nigger In Charge) role to the hilt for two hours made this movie well worthwhile.

B-Boys & Gangstas

Clockers

Written and Directed by Spike Lee
Starring Mekhi Phifer and Harvey Keitel

"Clockers" are black kids who work 'round tha clock selling crack cocaine. Richard Price's novel *Clockers* serves up a white cop battling these clockers on the rusted and cramped playgrounds of innercity Brooklyn. *Clockers* the movie, however, serves up the metaphoric Strike. He's an archetypal black man created by America, playing in the only playground he's allowed into — the underworld. Like most b-boyz, Strike is spiritually aged well beyond his youthful years; he's in the twilight of the precious few dayz that the inner city has set aside for him. His white doppelganger is Harvey Keitel's homicide detective, doing his best to squash this monster that society has constructed. On the planet Brooklyn, these two battle to meaningless stalemates, until their spent attempts are replaced by those of new pawns. As usual Spike's cinematic mirror reflects it all with poetry and motion. It is a must see.

***

In Too Deep

Directed by Michael Rymer
Starring Omar Epps, LL Cool J and Nia Long

The title says it all in this formulaic thriller. The film focuses on the battle between good and evil within the drug underworld of the streets on Cincinnati. A recent police academy graduate, Detective Jeff Cole, played by the always-watchable Omar Epps, believes that he was born to be an undercover agent. When he sets his sights on the crack kingpin known as God, played eerily evil by rapper LL Cool J, the battle begins.

God has his fingers in eighty percent of the city's crime, and no police officer on the city's force has ever been able to bring him down. But when Jeff Cole proves that he's up to the challenge after a few big busts, it looks like things are gonna change.

The screenwriters/producers of *In Too Deep*, Michael Henry Brown (*Dead Presidents*) and Paul Aaron, have said that they set out to not make a typical cop movie. They wanted to blur the lines between good and evil by having Epp's character — the good guy — become emotionally attached to the bad guy. Gee, what a novel concept.

With that said, what happens in the movie is just what they tried to avoid — a typical cop movie. That's not to say that the premise is not a good one, and in fact, a few years ago Mike Newell

(*Four Weddings and a Funeral*) made an amazing film with a similar premise — *Donnie Brasco* starring Johnny Depp and Al Pacino.

That film worked because we were allowed to feel the bond as it grew between the cop and the criminal. We actually empathized with the criminal (Pacino). No such luck in *In Too Deep*, as both Epps and LL both come off as arrogant and unlikeable, so we don't care for either of them. The cast, as is usually the case in these kinds of films, is extremely attractive, with the likes of Pam Grier, Nia Long, and Hill Harper. The soundtrack is booming, and the attitude is too cool. *In Too Deep* serves as nothing but an extended ad for the soundtrack album.

***

Sunset Park

Directed by Steve Gomer
Starring Rhea Perlman and Fredro Starr

At some point, it becomes pointless to make the critical observation that the idea behind a particular film is unoriginal, as just about every angle of telling stories has been exhausted. The only thing

to look forward to is some originality in the execution and energy of the paint-by-numbers storyline and characters.

The Bad News Bears did it with truly quirky and engaging characters, and *Dangerous Minds* did it by pumping its done-to-death high school drama with groovin' hip-hop jams that provided a whole new layer and subtext to an otherwise standard movie. *Sunset Park* is peculiar in that it doesn't even do a good imitation of one of these movies. It takes on a very bland and mediocre stance in its telling of the tried-and-true tale of losers becoming winners, of the outsider coach metamorphing "disadvantaged" kids into something beautiful and vice-versa.

All the set ups are there — rivalry over a high school sweetheart, a doped and dazed student headed for a downfall, a ladies man always on the hunt — but there is no execution or resolution for any of these. The sweetheart is simply dismissed as a tramp, the doped up kid just stops doing dope, and the ladies' man remains a ladies' man. All of this goes against the golden rule of moviemaking: drama is conflict. There is no conflict and thus no drama.

Rhea Perlman does a fair job of convincing us that she really is the character she plays, and Fredro Starr (of the rap group ONYX) gives a good rendition of the tough kid who's sweet on the inside. The rest of the "kids" (many are in their twenties) seem to be caricatures of what someone thinks inner city b-ball players are like, not what they actually are. The cinematography does its best to paint the picture, using the requisite palette of greys and browns as well as bleeding out any hint of color and vibrancy in order to underscore the grim theme of inner city hopelessness.

Sunset Park could've used more classroom scenes and at-home scenes to flesh out the characters so that the audience could relate and care about the players. It would seem that all they do is play basketball. When Perlman uses tenacity to deal with a teacher who is bullying one of her players, it's an effective scene with just the right amount of sweetness, and it allows us to care. This type of scene could have augmented the other subplots that are meandering through the movie and created a more balanced and realistic view of the people protrayed in this drama.

The would-be saving grace should be a bumping soundtrack to help the audience get through the ho-hum dramatics, but there is no luck here either, the promise of some killer grooves being only halfway delivered. Beats and songs that aid in the transition shots in the movie are kept on a short leash, only letting the urgent tracks go but so far, and like the movie as a whole, never letting it just flow.

***

Black Docs

An American Love Story

Directed by Jennifer Fox

A ten-hour PBS documentary/television series *An American Love Story* follows the Wilson-Sims family with an all-access pass to every nook and cranny of their lives. The family is made up of the parents Bill and Karen and their daughters Cicily and Chaney. Bill and Karen, an interracial couple (he's black, she's white), met and fell in love in 1967. It's been twenty-something years since they moved from Ohio to the racially mixed community of Flushing, Queens, New York. Their hope was that this multiracial community would be also racially tolerant.

However, during this time, New York City had become a hot bed of vicious racial politics and attacks. The ten-part series opens as the first episode follows the family as they travel to pick up their eldest daughter, Cicily from elite Colgate University where she struggles to fit in. It then goes on to document their trials and tribulations in trying to exist in America. Cicily goes to Africa for a semester and Karen is diagnosed with fibroid tumours.

The youngest daughter, twelve-year old Chaney, begins her first relationship with a boy. The middle shows, episodes five and seven, prove to be the most interesting as they show Karen going back to her "white trash" roots in a trailer park in Florida and Bill going back to his "black thug" roots in Marion, Ohio. In the last episodes Karen loses her job and can't find another one, so she slips into a period of depression just as Bill faces his drinking problem. It's heart-wrenching.

The last episode here nicely sums up Bill and Karen's turbulent existence by following them to their high school reunion where they joyfully and painfully confront the events and reasons that made them leave Ohio in the first place. *An American Love Story* has gone to the Sundance and Berlin film festivals before coming here to Hot Docs, so it obviously has its supporters. However, the series isn't interesting enough to warrant a ten-hour exploration.

The series is a copy of a groundbreaking film series that PBS made twenty-four years ago on a family in Santa Barbara called the Louds. That series wasn't very interesting, but because it was new — this whole idea of turning the camera onto everyday people to see their idiosyncrasies up close — it was dramatic.

The problem with *An American Love Story* is that it takes a structure that has been used already and a content (racial problems in America) that has been overdone beyond belief. What you come up with is hours of mostly uncompelling stuff. And in an age where the Discovery Channel, A&E, TLC, and a host of other cable channels are doing amazing documentaries simply as a matter of course, anyone entering this genre has got to come correct. This is not to say that *An American Love Story* is all bad — it does make some good and insightful points. After all, you're bound to find some compelling stuff if you shoot one thousand hours of footage over a five-year period of anything. But it's more an exercise in good editing than in good documentary filmmaking. See it, if just for the effort put into it.

***

A Great Day in Harlem

Directed by Jean Bach

Glancing through an average American history book, one notices that the historically significant photos seem to only give names to the white faces in the picture. The faces of color remain spectral and nameless, without identity, without a story.

In filmmaking, the story is the main thing —

what happened to whom, when, and where. Often it isn't a question of if there is a story, but rather where it is. Filmmakers Jean Bach and Matt Seig found in an old photograph a story and names — many names, big names. By deconstructing the mechanics, personalities, and history that resulted in a famous jazz picture, they made *A Great Day in Harlem*.

The photograph in question is a picture taken by Art Kane back in 1958. Art Kane, a respected art director, had never taken a professional photograph at this time, but he had been asked to contribute to a jazz issue of *Esquire* magazine. His idea was to gather a group of the leading jazz figures of the New York City jazz scene up in Harlem at ten o'clock one morning and take an all-star jazz photograph.

As is often the case with many documentaries, the more you dig, the more you find. They interviewed many of the surviving musicians and acquired delicious slivers of old jazz footage of the many performers who appeared in the picture. They taped wonderful reminisces of elderly Dizzy Gillespie and Art Blakey. Bach and Seig not only provided a cute anecdotal backstory, but they give a loving, praise-like history lesson of jazz personalities as well.

As *A Great Day in Harlem* winds down, some vintage black and white film footage of jazz performances are woven with insightful 8mm shots from the actual day of the photograph as well as abrasively lit video images of the surviving "jazz masters" giving testimonials and praising each other. It's wonderful to see jazz paying homage to itself, with Art Blakey singing the praises of Thelonious Monk, or Dizzy modestly deferring to the talents of Chubby Jackson.

The story that has been captured is a story of a gathering, not only a physical gathering which the filmmakers seem more concerned with, but more importantly, a spiritual gathering. Though the film doesn't totally get across the quivering nostalgia that it attempts, it does give names and stories to people who America has often ignored.

***

Standing in the Shadows of Motown

Directed by Paul Justman
Written by Allan Slutsky

Standing in the Shadows of Motown will make you cry; in a good way. It will take you back to a time whether you are of that time or not, that's how powerful this documentary is. This movie is a very well made documentary about the musicians that provided the brilliant musical soundscapes for the likes of Smokey Robinson, the Supremes, Marvin Gaye, etc. Collectively this group of musicians who played on more top ten hits than the Beatles, the Rolling Stones and Elvis Presly combined, dubbed themselves, The Funk Brothers.

And in what amounts to nothing short of share-cropping, these talented and beautiful artists gave their all to Berry Gordy and produced some of the greatest music of the 20th century. By providing steady work but minimal pay to these marginalised yet brilliant black musicians in the 60's, Berry Gordy was able to work the Funk Brothers to death, having them record with every Motown act on an almost daily basis.

Standing in the Shadows of Motown tells the Funk Brother's story, combining exclusive interviews, archival footage, re-enactments, reminiscences, and funky new performances of old Motown standards by the reunited Funk Brothers and such contemporary music stars as Joan Osbourne, Ben Harper and Michelle Ndegeocello.

What the film does well is to vividly bring to life a time and place and the people who where there. Through archival footage and re-enactments, the director, Paul Justman makes us feel as if we knew these great musical warriors who have passed on; People like Benny "Papa Zita" Benjamin, James "Igor" Jamerson, and Eddie "Bongo" Brown. So

much so that when the remaining Funk Brothers stage a reunion concert and they precede that by bring out large photos of the band members who have died, you can't help but weep.

The movie could have easily been a long bitch session about how Berry Gordy abandoned the heart and soul of these Detroit musicians for the glitz and glamour of Hollywood, but it doesn't. Rather, it chooses to look at what was good about those times — love, respect and friendship. It's an outstanding movie — go see it.

***

Life & Debt

Directed by Stephanie Black

It was hard for me not to like Stephanie Black's *Life & Debt*. First of all, unlike most documentaries that we see today, Black shot her film on lush 35mm rather than the flat bloodless look of video. Not only that, but she uses some amazing DPs, including Spike Lee's DP extraordinaire Malik Sayeed. And on top of it all, she frames the narrative of Life & Debt with Jamaica Kincaid's eloquent and condemning writing from her anti-colonial classic *A*

Small Place.

Life & Debt sets out to be an exposé of the International Monetary Fund's involvement and culpability in Jamaica's economic woes, and in doing that, accusing the IMF of being involved in the financial misery of all third world countries.

Having grown up in the post-colonial West Indies, the spectre of the big bad first world is a potent one, and I'm sure that Black's heavy handed narrative style will initially strike a chord with people with the first-hand experience of living in the Caribbean. She makes her one-sided argument against the IMF go down easier by continuously heaping on healthy servings of favourite songs.

With a soundtrack that includes everything from Harry Belafonte's "Day-O/Banana Boat Song" to Bob Marley's de facto third world anthem "One Love," you can't help but be on the side of the 'little people.' And like any good Hollywood movie you need a definitive face to put on evil, someone that the audience can root against.

Amazingly, the director provides IMF spokesman Stanley Fischer. A powerful organization like the IMF usually holds its cards close, so it is almost surreal that Black gets Mr. Fischer on camera pretty much 'hanging' himself. Granted, she does splice together Fischer toeing the IMF party line with clips of former Jamaican PM Michael Manley denouncing IMF policy. With the breezy Manley being a million times more charismatic than the stuffy shirt Fischer, the director has us where she wants us again.

Incidentally, it was director Stephanie Black's former work on Sesame Street (she was a segment producer) that made her appear "safe" to the IMF and made it possible for her to even to get the interview with Fischer. And though most western critics have swallowed *Life & Debt* hook, line and sinker, it's ironically the Jamaican press that has been the most critical of the doc.

The Jamaican Gleaner dismisses *Life and Debt* as one-sided and of trying to absolve Jamaica of any culpability in her own downfall. They are also quick to point out that it was Manley's own economic missteps and policies that forced Jamaica into the 'clutches' of the IMF in the first place. But with all of that said, the documentary *Life and Debt*, despite its ideological aspirations, is more of an artistic rather than political triumph.

***

Raisin' Kane: A Rapumentary

Directed by Allison Duke

In *Raisin' Kane*, the classic David and Goliath battle story is played out with lyrics and beats as the weapons in this age-old clash. While hip-hop has been embraced by the mainstream as the most influential youth culture, the artists themselves are still struggling for respect.

Alison Duke's directorial debut *Raisin' Kane* is a gutsy process-doc that crackles with energy as it takes us into the never-before-seen world of independent hip-hop artists Citizen Kane during a critical turning point in their history — as they drop their first CD. The energy is raw and real as their dreams come up against the realities of the music biz.

Duke's journey to make her directorial debut was not a typical one. She earned a Master's Degree in Kinetics before she shifted gears and began writing social commentary in the area of music for local magazines. Duke quickly realized that despite the number of black artists who were making music videos, there were few black producers and directors. In 1996, she and her partners formed a production company where Duke produced and direct- ed videos and produced a feature film.

With *Raisin' Kane: a Rapumentary*, Duke introduces a fresh perception of the young black male as enterprising entrepreneur. The members of Citizen Kane have been friends since kindergarten and reveal the realities of growing up in a Canadian ghetto. To understand them, it is important to understand where they're from.

The public housing high-rises that enclose the world where these young black men came of age look like prisons. Here, high unemployment and low-cost housing equals no hope or dreams in the eyes of the kids who live there. Citizen Kane is comprised of three men: Adrian Perry ("Aje"), a university grad who has already escaped the neighborhood, but manages the band in hopes of trading in his government job for showbiz; Jeff Duke ("Spade"), a brooding, first-generation Canadian, who is hell bent on providing a better life for his daughter and does his best to navigate the treacherous industry demands; and his partner, Rob Parish ("Blye"), a fiery-tempered Nova Scotian whose "ghetto credo" is living one day at a time, and who has no time for the business bull.

Together they must battle and overcome an amalgamation of elements: big record companies, shady distribution organizations, little radio play, and a general indifference to the most powerful cultural youth movement of our time — hip-hop. More than anything, the film wants the world to hear what the segment of society that Citizen Kane represents has to say.

Interviews with hip-hop experts — from cultural critic Nelson George and hip-hop recording artist Michie Mee to the kids from the projects — allow the film to convey a genuine understanding of the living, breathing, real people behind the slick facade that hip-hop puts forth. But the film is not just a story about overcoming insurmountable odds: it's also about something more magical. It shows a method to the madness of artists who are hell-bent on being heard over the din of an indifferent world.

***

A Season of Change

Directed by Robert Gervais and Michael Kronish

A Season of Change is a documentary by Canadian filmmakers Robert Gervais and Michael Kronish that looks at Jackie Robinson's 1946 season with the Montreal Royals. This shattered the color barrier in baseball and thus anticipated the civil rights movement in the US.

The filmmakers have skillfully used rare archival footage, present-day taped interviews, and clever reconstructed scenes to tell not only the story of the first black player in professional baseball, but more significantly the story about a shift in the thinking of society as a whole, with regards to race.

A Season of Change is at its best when it weaves Jackie Robinson's tale of individual courage with the social commentary of civil rights, as well as with the historical/ social significance and inner workings of the city of Montreal in the forties. The documentary is a welcomed addition to the legend of Jackie Robinson, and it is one that throws light on a period of Robinson's life that is often unobserved.

***

Vintage: Families of Value

Directed by Thomas Allen Harris

At one point during *Vintage*, the director's father tells a story about how in the South, parents would often teach their sons how to survive a lynching by catching the rope under their Adams apple and how one family's son died one day while practicing this. He concludes by saying that the family simply hid their pain and never mentioned it again.

The tragic irony that this story expresses says a lot about *Vintage* and a lot about some of the self-inflicted demons that this black family deals with on a daily basis yet no one seems to mention. This is quite evident in the scenes with Harris as he tries to re-establish ties with his estranged father where they both beat around the emotional bush, never really saying what needs to be said. When Harris eventually says some of what's on his mind, the father rejects him again.

The gay, gifted, and black siblings that *Vintage* profiles do much to add a new dimension to the tired image of the black family that is often offered by the media. The director, Thomas Allen Harris, delivers up three sets of siblings: Anni, Adrian, and Anita, three sisters all attracted to women; Paul and Vanessa, a very femme and downtown fag and his very proud-to-be-butch sister; and finally, Lyle and Thomas, two boyish and openly gay black men. Within each set, Harris reveals the intellectual and even spiritual machinations that drive these individuals. Because of the close emotional proximity that families exist in, silent gratitude and silent appreciation often take the place of actual voiced sentiments.

When the gay Paul opens up and tells how he wished his sister Vanessa would have been more discreet with her butchness, the director Harris throws up a surreal sequence in which Paul plays a damsel and Vannessa plays a tuxedo clad Casanova.

It's hilarious yet unnervingly insightful.

The three lesbian sisters, Anni, Adrian, and Anita, amalgamate their thoughts on sexuality, spirituality, and abuse to give one of the most honest, no-holds-barred intimations of sexual self-analysis ever seen on film. One of the sisters goes on to sum up the irrationality of the world today by declaring that "the world is in the throes of patriarchy, and the earth is out of balance."

Despite technical shortcomings, *Vintage* provides an invaluable record of an aspect of the modern family and community. It adds yet some more of the much-needed strokes to the ever-evolving media canvas that depicts the black family and thus the black individual.

***

Our Planet Africa

Asientos

Directed by Francois Woukoache

In a cluttered room, a tilted television beams footage of white photojournalists converging on Rwandan war victims, clicking away at the real life pain as if it were a local press conference.

With such surreal scenes, Francois Woukoache's *Asientos* constructs a visual African journey from the barbaric slave trade up to the brutality of Africa today. With unsettling "skinscapes" and winding shots of gruesome icons like shackles, slave ship blueprints, and maps, the film paints a sinister connection between old and new Africa.

***

Le Franc

Directed by Djibil Diop Mambety

When it comes to blending the strange and iconic structures of the fable with the magical expression of motion picture, none have done it with quite the quirkiness that African cinema has. Djibril Mambety's short film *Le Franc* is a great example of the amalgamation of the two forms of story telling. The fundamental notion is that when the complexities of a film are stripped away it simply reveals a character on a journey to have a need fulfilled. This is more than evident in *Le Franc*. *Le Franc* begins, as all good fables do, in the morning.

Marigo, our anti-hero, is a down but not-quite-out Senegalese musician. He is awoken by the hollering of his "tenement lordess" roaring for her unpaid rent money. This sets our Afro-Chaplinesque friend on his way.

The camera plays a curious peeping tom as we get a look into every nook and cranny of the tiny village, a comic yet tragic image of life here. Marigo gravitates into town where he takes a beatdown as well as a lottery ticket from a midget. As any lazy shiftless Negro would do, Marigo puts total faith and hope into the much sought after instant gratification that the lottery ticket represents. He goes back to his pad and pastes it to his door for safekeeping.

Of course, Marigo's ticket number comes in and so begins his trek to the lottery office, front door et al. It is hard not to see some sort of economic metaphor for Africa's present financial straits within Marigo's adventure, as throughout the film the camera never lets us forget about the quivering poverty that Marigo is trying to elude, with shots of urban Africa at its polluted and shoddy worst. Like Antonioni's decaying, rotting Rome, Mambety, too, forgoes glimpses of a lush and stunning Senegal for a rather bitter dirty, concrete, and littered Senegal. Like Chaplin's Little Tramp, we can't help but root for this likeable dreamer as Marigo constantly drifts in and out of his fantasy realm. When the gorgeous receptionist at the lottery office tells Marigo that the claim numbers for his cache of cash are on the back of the ticket which is glued tight to his door, the whole story seems about to collapse under the irony.

This so-close-but-yet-so-far gimmick seems to be a perfect bittersweet ending to this journey. Nevertheless, Mambety snatches our hero from his impending doom and despair by having Marigo fling himself, door et al, into the sea in a cathartic 'curses to the gods scene.

***

Karmen

"Love is a vagabond child who knows no laws."
      —Karmen

Directed by Joseph Ramaka
Starring Djeinaba Diop Gai

Drum beats and sex: that's what pushes this movie to its foregone conclusion. And at some point in the film, the drum and the sex become one.

This movie is incredibly sexy. That's the first thing that hits you about this Senegalese retelling of Bizet's opera *Carmen*. It smolders with sexuality and desire. As a matter of fact, the logo for the movie's press kit is an inviting silhouette of a black female's buttocks, presumably Karmens'.

Like all the film interpretations of Bizet's most famous work — fifty-two at last account — the emotional spirit that drives the piece is the frustration that Karmen has with the constraints of society coupled with the frustrations that her suitors feel at not being able to possess their mercurial lover. Otto Preminger's audacious "all black" *Carmen* and director Joseph Ramaka's *Karmen* versions are the most imaginative interpretations of this timeless story.

Ramaka goes one step further than Premminger by bringing to the surface the latent homoerotic subtext that seems to exist in most takes on *Carmen* but is never really explored. As a matter of fact, Karmen's true love in this film is a butchy female prison guard captain. Their sweaty late night tryst is one of the sexiest things you'll see on film all year. By setting the story in a fairy talesque seaside African village, Ramaka makes the well-worn story his own. And by seemingly being given a decent budget, he's allowed to be lush with his set pieces, and the film is not bogged down with shoddy production value.

The production sparkles like any big-budget Euro film. This "African" *Karmen* opens up with a spectacular dance sequence amidst the ghosts of slavery in the infamous slave castle of Goree Island. The castle is now a female prison, and the prisoners are rebelling in the only way that characters rebel in a musical – by staging an intense dance routine.

The ringleader is Karmen, played by stunning newcomer Djeinaba Diop Gai who brings ferocious feline sexuality to her character. Karmen's sensual gyrations are not lost on the warden, Aneglique, and Karmen is summoned to the warden's quarters later that night. So with the warden sated by Karmen's sexual affections, Karmen escapes, and the movie begins its narrative arc toward Karmen's ultimate demise.

Like any truly free character, she must die for society's sins. For those unfamiliar with the storyline of Bizet's *Carmen*, this Nubian one will not help you along at all. The story is almost non-existent and disjointed at best. But despite its structural flaws,

the film works incredibly well as an art piece. It's a well-choreographed and beautifully-staged loose take on a classic tale. Much in the way that *Moulin Rouge* wins you over with its sheer zeal, so does Ramaka's *Karmen* seduce you. It does so with its smoldering, enticing abandon, which is precisely what makes its lead character seductive to so many directors.

***

Mandela

Directed by Angus Gibson

At the risk of sounding clichéd, documentary biographies usually fall into two categories: good and not so good. Mandela is definitely good, particularly in the light of the fact that the South African struggle has been so well documented and covered by the Western media.

This all makes the undeniable appeal of this film all the more compelling. Good documentaries usually succeed because of the X factor — introducing the audience to something that is unknown and new. But seeing as Mandela has been such a media-darling cum celebrity for decades, the documentary could not depend on that element.

What this film does in order to succeed is to blend style and substance so deftly that the concoction mesmerizes us as it educates us. Many docs on the situation in South Africa and apartheid are so overtly good versus evil — black natives good, white interlopers bad — that there is no real friction, no real story. The evils of the apartheid system in South Africa are usually too undeniable to draw one in.

But what this film's creative forces (forces that include Jonathan Demme and Island Pictures) do is to show Mandela for what he really is — not a victim, but a hero. As a young·man, the charismatic Mandela fled home to avoid an arranged marriage, and he trained as a boxer before becoming a lawyer: a Renaissance man, if ever there was one. That is the Mandela that we are presented with.

By having Mandela himself act as a sort of narrator for the piece, his integrity and sincerity do much in making the horrors of this crime against humanity palatable. And by tracing Mandela's heritage and story with that of his people, the filmmakers create a powerful narrative force to ensnare the audience.

Though the piece runs at a perfect hour, the rise, fall, and rise story arc that Mandela's story takes is so rich, layered, and dense with personal observations of Mandela and social observation of the stormy political climate of modern South Africa

that even at an hour, the presentation has an undeniable spiritual gravity.

The filmmakers also do well in avoiding the CNN school of documentary storytelling by employing everything from blue-tinged talking head-shots of Mandela to mixing groovy Johnny Clegg tunes with frightening black-and-white footage of the South African militia on horseback in the fifties.

However, despite all the nobility and stature that the film affords Mandela, it does fail to present Mandela as a simple man. However, maybe as his sister says in the closing of the programme, 'My brother was not simply born for to embrace and aid our family, but to embrace and aid a whole country. So unlike the typical Hollywood hero, maybe there is no simplicity to this real life hero after all.

***

When the Stars Meet the Sea/ Quand Les Etoiles Rencontrent La Mer

Directed by Raymond Rajaonarivelo

A splendidly photographed Madagascar is the canvas upon which this Oedipal tale is played out.

In Rajaonarivelo's *When the Stars Meet the Sea*, a botched ritual creates outcasts of a childless woman and her crippled son, condemning them to a bleak life on the fringes. When the son grows up and finds that the flawed ritual gave him mythic powers, he journeys back to the village to find out who he really is.

***

Woubi Cheri

Directed by Laurent Bocahut

Woubi Cheri is a sixty-two minute documentary from the Ivory Coast by Philip Brooks and Laurent Bocahut. *Woubi* is a funny and ribald piece about gender pioneers constructing a distinct homosexual identity. "Woubi" is actually the term given to the transvestites who live in the villages of the Ivory Coast. They are very open about their gender bending and often sleep with married men who have separate lives as husbands and fathers. These men are called "yossis".

Though the film offers some interesting insights into African sexual politics and how it has changed and differs from Western perceptions of sexuality,

over all it still lacks the "oomph" that such documentaries usually deliver. Perhaps if this piece were seen ten years earlier it would be more profound, but with films like Isaac Julien's *Darker Shade of Black* and the New York film *Paris is Burning* already having dealt with similar themes in a more electric and riveting fashion, *Woubi Cheri* unfortunately gives the viewer of sense of dÉja vu. Despite this, it still remains a well-crafted look into a part of the African psyche that we rarely, if ever, see.

***

La Vie Sur Terre/ Life on Earth

Written & Directed by Abderrahmane Sissako

With the millennium fast approaching, artists of all disciplines are all scrambling to illustrate their unique take on what it means. Abderrahmane Sissako of Mali forgoes the typical apocalyptic vision of the year 2000 and instead gives an elegant meditation on New Year's Eve 1999 as observed in a tiny, dusty village in Mali.

The golden sandy landscape is stunningly shot, and the skin tones of the Africans possess real visual gravity when in close-up. Throughout the film an archaic transistor radio crackles with a blow-by-blow report from Paris on how the millennium eve is being celebrated there. It's a drunken, technological orgy to be sure. Sissako skilfully juxtaposes that report from urban Europe with the slowness of the goings-on in this small village where there still is only one phone.

The height of a beautiful young African woman's day is to have her picture taken by the lone antiquated camera in the village. Sissako ties all these philosophical paradoxes up beautifully with a narration by Martiniquais poet Aime Cesaire, whose anticolonialist poetry points to the European industrial revolution as the reason that Africa lags behind industrially to this day. As the poem goes, "I put my ear to the ground and heard tomorrow pass."

Tha Birth of a new Black Film Criticism

It's been roughly one hundred years since the birth of cinema and much has been written about its influence on society, so much so that literary film criticism has become a genre in and of itself. Like any genre, film criticism remanifests itself in several subgenres. Whether it's the brainy musings of Pauline Kael or the appealing film takes of Roger Ebert, the books keep coming.

Recently we have seen the release of books skewed to an urban audience with film criticism by urban pop culture critics: bell hooks (*Reel to Real*), Nelson George (*Blackface*), and Donald Bogle (*Blacks in American Films and Television*). Having reviewed films for over the last ten years in *The Hilltop* (Howard U.'s school paper), *FUSE* magazine, and *Word* magazine, a Toronto-based urban magazine, I see that there is an audience for a specific urban pop culture take and retake on film.

My idea was to assemble an exciting and ecc-electic urban group of film lovers with unique voices and insightful prespectives on life and art. They would then be locked in a room with a big screen TV, a bunch of DVDs, and be asked to devour and riff on our generation's important films: the good, the bad, and the ugly.

The members who made up this funky think tank

are not professional film critics or film makers — they're just regular folk who are as entitled to an opinion as any thumbs up television pundit.

Our panel wishes to retain their anonymity — it's the films' qualifications that matter, not the viewers' — and go by the following aliases: Acid, Sweet Bwaoy, Don Cash (a.k.a. Rob Money), Indu, and Sassy Am.

Our mission with this book is to bumrush the urban films that have been served to us since the birth of the hip-hop generation. Like a literary equivalent of ABC's Politically Incorrect crossed with Mystery Science Theatre 3000, we want to take these four diverse voices and synthesize them into a funky flowing collective articulation about the pop cultural effects of these movies.

Part 3:
Tha Riffs and Rantz

Tha Riffs and Rantz

Preface

The following films are grouped in pairs, not for straight-up comparisons but as an exercise to look at these films when counterpointed alongside a film with similar themes but from a different era, culture, or point of view. For example, Beat Street is a fictional account of the early days of hip-hop in New York City. The counterpoint film is The Show, a documentary about where modern hip-hop is fifteen years after Beat Street's focused time. Together we riff on how the two films both reinforce and dispute each other's ideas.

1.) Back in tha Day

BEAT STREET vs THE SHOW

A.) *Beat Street* (1984)

Directed by: Stan Lathan

Written by: Andy Davis (III) & David Gilbert

Outline: An aspiring D.J. from the South Bronx tries to get his big break in the early hip-hop club scene.

With: Rae Dawn Chong, Guy Davis, and Mary Alice

B.) *The Show* (1995)

Directed by: Brian Robbins

Outline: A documentary about the culture of hip-hop with a focus on Wu Tang, Craig G, and Snoop Dogg.

With: The Notorious B.I.G, Method Man, and Slick Rick

ACID

So what differences did you guys see [comparing The Show to Beat Street]?

DON CASH

It was more about where they were. And it was obviously something that if you were down with Russell Simmons or Rush Management, then you were down, you got to be in the movie. And if you weren't, then you didn't exist in hip-hop. So you can't really say that The Show was like a comprehensive overview, and I didn't even really get the feeling of it as a true take on the times [1996].

However, as a document of where hip-hop culture was in 1984, I think Beat Street was far more effective. . . I know the exact time that the documentary [The Show] was made. I remember everything about it, and I was living in NYC at the time, and I didn't really see anything in The Show that really like struck me as poignant or made me nostalgic for that time. . .

SWEET BWAOY

What struck me most about The Show is that some of the key figures from the Beat Street era were Afrika Bambata [and] Cool Herc when they were young and in their prime, but then when you see them 12 years later in The Show. They're like our dads and shit. They're all sitting around that freakin' desk, discussing things or whatever, but none of them actually started freestyling with each other.

ACID

Don Cash makes a good point about one of the narrative journeys. Like in Beat Street, it's sort of like the characters were genuinely excited just to go and play records for, like, crowds in an abandoned brownstone, right? They're plugging in their gear illegally into the light post, and that was it, party was on. And those guys — those kids from the Bronx in the early 80s — lived for it right. And you kinda really got that. I mean, it's illustrated so well in the story and performances that they lived to be out there for the breaking, for the graffiti, for the music — this new music and culture that was being created right before their eyes.

And then in the documentary The Show, DMC of Run DMC kind of echoes that buzz in the hip-hop world in the 80s when he says, "You know, even if I was writing for myself, even if I was working for the post office, I'd still be writing rhymes." I kinda liked that sense of commitment to the art not the cash. Think about the journey of those early hip-hoppers performing for tiny but enthused crowds in abandoned buildings in the Bronx in Beat Street, and [then] go all the way to twelve, thirteen years later to the era of The Show documenting Wutang's tour in Japan performing for thousands of Japanese kids who don't even speak English.

DON CASH

One thing that was interesting in the two films [is that] I don't think that the phrase 'a million dollars' was used at all in Beat Street, but, damn, we must have heard the term 'a million dollars' 150 times in The Show. So you can see how the whole money thing had really taken over by the mid-90s, and you could see that it takes away from the happiness involved in making music. It wouldn't be acceptable to hip-hop artists today to play in front of 25 people in an abandoned Bronx warehouse. And in Beat Street that's what it was all about, it was all about these guys and how they lived for their art even though they weren't famous artists.

ACID

I think it underscores Don Cash's theory that hip-hop pretty much died at some point in the mid- to late 90s. You're right because there was no joy in anybody's face; they all looked like they were at a funeral or something. I mean, even Method Man, and l love Wutang, but they all just talked about meeting promo obligations, being on time for interviews, and stuff, and there was no talk of making rhymes, making music.

SWEET BWAOY

Yeah, you think they'd be like freestyling on the tour bus.

DON CASH

Oh yeah, there was a part in The Show when they touched on writing rhymes and shit. The one time when we followed Treach [Naughty By Nature] as he walked through his old neighborhood [and] was talking about the house he was living in at the time, and you could tell he was really nostalgic about this old house where he wrote all the songs from that first Naughty By Nature album. . . But that's probably the only time that you really saw that sort of sincerity in The Show.

ACID

What did you think aesthetically about The Show?

DON CASH

It's hard to say. I think that as a documentary, I didn't like the concert scenes. . .

ACID

Yeah, you're right. It doesn't go wild and shit, it doesn't go all cinema verite and just get whatever the camera gets, warts and all — it's pretty cosmetic. But the one interesting thing about The Show is that even though it's a documentary, it played in theatres, and it actually made some money. Which is kind of amazing because documentaries don't usually have theatrical releases. So can you today make sense of why in '95 everyone would rush out and go see this movie?

DON CASH

Because that was the height of the no hip-hop show era. Hardly any hip-hop bands were going on tour, and when bands like Wu [Tang Clan] would do a show, only two guys from the group would show. Because hip-hop had such a bad reputation, venues were too afraid to rent them stages and shit.

ACID

Well, what about Beat Street. How'd that movie touch you?

SWEET BWAOY

I thought Beat Street was so epic when I first saw it. I remember seeing it as a kid, but I think I'd have to go through therapy to figure out exactly why. I think when I went to go see that film it was like more of an escapist sort of thing . . . It was a whole event. And this is a movie that represented how I wanted to live when I was a kid. But to see it now, it doesn't have the relevance that it did back then. Now I have no interest in freakin' linking up with some breakdancers to battle on the freakin' subway. But when I was a kid, I remember thinking in school that as soon as recess hits, we're gonna freakin' settle some beef, we're gonna spin it out on a freakin' enzyme cardboard thing. . .

ACID

Yeah. . . I remember that New York City had such an appeal then — you just thought that was the Mecca for young urban black culture. Even looking at the photography of Beat Street now, it's so gritty, so for its time, it must have come across as really genuine. And I remember seeing it back then and identifying with that little kid, Kenny's brother Henry, growing up in the city. He's not the lead, but he really is the most empathetic character in there.

DON CASH

Yeah, that was the character that I most identified with. He was, like, the foreshadowing of the golden age of hip-hop. That's the real b-boy element right there, you know — it's just like looking at Elvis in black leather and black hair. It's like, you wanna know what a b-boy looks like, watch the little brother in Beat Street.

He makes it real. And the good part is the other actors realize that, and they gave him his space, and they definitely followed his lead, so that made something that could have been really bad really good. And it was good to see black people making hip-hop style music and actually caring about the art. 'Cause you know, it's gotten to such a pathetic

point with hip-hop music these days that it's just good to see that. Not like in The Show, which is all about making money.

ACID

Yeah, but The Show also captures the charisma of hip-hop today. Like, Method Man's a big star now, and he comes across as such in The Show, kind of the way the kid Henry does in Beat Street. Method Man could be like that kid years later. And also Biggie — I mean, I wasn't always a Biggie fan, but seeing him onscreen in The Show now, you really see that he has presence. I understand his appeal. So The Show does succeed in some ways.

I think we all understand that there's a major West Indian influence in hip-hop that is sometimes recognized, sometimes not. And I just love the scenes where evidence of that influence comes out. Like, when we see Biggie, and he's talking about growing up on the streets of Brooklyn, and he sounds like the all-American b-boy, and then they show his mom, and his mom's got this thick Jamaican accent, and we understand where Biggie is coming from.

DON CASH

It is hip-hop; there's the proof: Jamaican mom.

ACID

Yeah, it does say something about hip-hop in

the sense that Biggie's an immigrant, like he came to and he became Brooklyn. Like this is a kid from Jamaica who epitomized Brooklyn, you know what I mean? And epitomized hip-hop you know.

DON CASH

Well there's a lot of Biggies walking around Toronto. People just don't know it yet, but hopefully they will soon. And that's the good thing about hip-hop dying — hip-hop is too New York-centric, and I think that in the end, that's what's killing it. It's not possible to keep it in New York anymore. And that's something that you don't see in The Show, this idea that hip-hop's a lot bigger than what they showed there, and that, you know, the ideas of people who are into hip-hop today — their ideas are bigger than hip-hop.

DON CASH

I don't think it's necessarily a bad thing. I mean you can't make your own tradition if you're just trying to follow what somebody else did.

2.) Girls Ain't Nothin' But Trouble

A.) *Love & Basketball* (2000)

Written & Directed by: Gina Prince-Bythewood

Outline: When 11-year-old tomboy Monica moves next door to young b-baller Quincy, a love affair that spans fifteen years begins.

With: Omar Epps, Sanaa Lathan, and Alfre Woodard

B.) *Baby Boy* (2001)

Written & Directed by: John Singleton

Outline: A raw coming-of-age/arrested development movie set in present day South Central L.A.

With: Tyrese, Taraji P. Henson, and Omar Gooding.

BABY BOY vs LOVE AND BASKET-BALL

ACID

Which one did you like the most and why?

INDU

Love and Basketball — I much preferred Love and Basketball, just because the story's more compelling. I was able to identify with the actors. I felt compassion for them. . . I think the fact that it was directed by a woman really makes a difference in the illustration of emotions.

ACID

Sexuality is a big part of both of these movies and sexual relationships are. Do you see a vast difference in the way that sexuality and the sex act was dealt with in Love and Basketball as opposed to Baby Boy?

INDU

I just think that the depictions of a loving sexual relationship in Love and Basketball was more about love than the sexual relationships in Baby Boy. Baby Boy had love but there was always so much anger as well that was being portrayed. And that just turned me off.

ACID

You're right — the movie Baby Boy does have a real underlying layer of anger in it, especially in the depiction of the sex act. And the two leads, Jody and Yvette, they were almost, like, sex-mad in it.

INDU

Yeah, it was really graphic, particularly that scene in Baby Boy where they've just had that huge fight. She's so upset and he's just punched her. . .. She's so upset. He takes her to the bedroom and he goes down on her. She's crying as he's bringing her to orgasm. And all one can think [is], "Is this all he knows in terms of comforting another person and apologizing?" Like, 'Oh, baby, I'm really sorry — let me make you come.'

ACID

I actually thought that was a really interesting scene and it's a scene that you don't see in movies or at least in American films, and I think it's a scene that plays many times in relationships, don't you think?

It was like the first time he hit her, and she was obviously in emotional and physical pain because there was a line that had been crossed in the relationship, some trust had been lost. But he doesn't know how to comfort her. It's sort of like when the movie opens up with her coming from having what seems to be yet another abortion, and he takes her home and, you know, he does a very pedestrian offer of, 'Do you need anything?' She says no and he's like, 'Okay, I'm goingÖ' He doesn't really know how to comfort her. And then at that point, when he hits her, she really needs comforting, and the only thing he can do is to go down on her, perform oral sex on her. But I thought [that it was such] a powerful scene because in her head — I mean, again, it's from a male point of view — but the scene is so full of conflicting emotion and imagery that is powerful. While she's crying, she's in pain, he's also bringing her to orgasm at the same time in this particularly intimate fashion and we flash — or rather the director puts us inside her head — and there's this montage of marriage and positive, hopeful stuff, as if to say, 'This is how women or girls in this situation rationalize.' It's like, you know, 'It's all okay 'cause we'll be married some day.'

INDU

I found it really, really disturbing and obviously this character, Mr. Baby Boy, he's so incomplete, like he doesn't know how to emotionally relate to people. He's immature. He's irresponsible. He doesn't really know what he wants in life and he can't really connect with the people around him.

ACID

One thing I thought about Baby Boy the first time I saw it was that this is a really powerful film. And then after it had been out for a while, a lot of people I know were saying that they didn't like, but now watching it again many months later, I still think that it captures something powerful.

INDU

Such an angry, angry film.

ACID

It is. And I guess watching it in the same sitting as Love and Basketball, which is such a more gentle film in which the few times that the sex act is depicted in Love and Basketball, it's very loving and soft. Like a vagina. (LAUGHTER)

It could be the female director . . . over-romanticizing.

INDU

Possibly, but you know, she doesn't totally do that. I mean, she does depict a relationship that Quincy's [Omar Epps] has had, this extramarital affair, and so I think she gives multiple perspectives on the kinds of relationships that men and women will have.

ACID

One thing I thought that both directors built up in common was this strained parent-child relationship. They both dealt with it. And the one in Baby Boy was much more sensual, like one of the main story lines was about this boy Jody and his mom.

INDU

And this boy Jody and his own children as well.

ACID

Exactly. And it was really powerful, but I actually liked the gentle subtlety of the way that Love and Basketball dealt with the same parent-child [relationship]. I think [there is] a certain universality about this issue is that you don't often see in movies about mothers and daughters. I thought it was quite well done the bittersweet relationship between the mom [Alfre Woodard] and the daughter, Monica [Sanaa Lathan].

INDU

Well, [what] I think — without being stereotypical about black films from the nineties — is that the father-son and the mother-son relationship has really been depicted extensively, while the mother-daughter relationship hasn't been shown as much.

I also really liked the relationship between the two sisters in Love and Basketball. There was something really nice there.

The non-competitive nature of the relationship between Monica and her sister was really sweet. Even at the end, you know, her sister's there with her kid, and all of the women in the family are together, just kind of hanging out. I just thought it was really nice to see a non-competitive relationship between two women 'cause so often you'll see sisters being complete rivals and especially sisters that are so different from each other, as these two sisters were.

And one was like the beauty queen, but they were both really connected and that was really nice to see.

ACID

It actually was nice. Like, just the scenes of the older sister, the beauty queen braiding Monica's hair and stuff.

And though that line about the pearls in Love and Basketball was cheesy, it works. The one where Monica's all dolled up for the first time in her life 'cause she's going to the prom, and Mom looks at her tomboy daughter, finally prissed up for the first time, and she says to the older sister, 'Get your grandmother's pearls' [so Monica can wear them]. It's something cheesy, but [there's] something quite lovely about it.

INDU

It's interesting that Love and Basketball has these traditional sort of families being depicted of Mom and Dad and the kids in these nice houses in the 'burbs, but Baby Boy has, I guess, a newer kind of family being shown. Baby Boy and his mom — I mean, it was almost like a brother-sister relationship. Almost, but not entirely.

ACID

Both of these movies are set in California, but within different classes, obviously. Like, Love and Basketball is very much upper class.

INDU

Upper-middle class.

But it was weird because I found that the production design of the people's homes in Baby Boy, I didn't find those to be working class homes. They looked like really nice, middle class homes.

Well even the neighbourhoods in Baby Boy looked really nice. I mean, okay, then there were like drive-by shootings, so, you know, take that with a grain of salt. But . . . people weren't like totally down-and-out either, [so] they obviously worked hard and had made strides in their life, and I thought that was kind of cool.

ACID

What do you think the director in Baby Boy was saying about black sexuality?

I think that sometimes the black sex is too much sometimes. For example, the scene were Yvette is missing Jody, and she's talking to her girlfriend on the phone and then, totally out of the blue, her girlfriend's boyfriend comes up from behind and starts doing this girl from behind.

INDU

No, no, no — I don't think this woman had her boyfriend come and do her from behind. He obviously could not deal with the fact that the attention was taken away from him for one millisecond, and then he decides that he's going to come and claim her attention by fucking her from behind. It's another comment on the childlike nature that Singleton is dealing with in his story, in his characters.

ACID

Anger and sex.

INDU

And mistrust and the willingness to be at each other's throats. And I mean, it's kind of a sad portrayal of these people . . . hopefully this is all a figment of John Singleton's imagination, 'cause I would hate to think that people live their lives that way.

[He's] totally whiny. Almost impotent in his inability to sort of move on. And you know, there were moments where he just has, like, no ability to look at himself critically and just see, like, what the fuck and I doing with my life. And then he had other moments where it was really clear that he could see what was happening and he was trying to kind of work through stuff. But for the most part he was just totally immature.

ACID

The director totally illustrated that when this "father figure," his mom's boyfriend, moves into the house. [He's] this kind of huge, virile man played by Ving Rhames. And all of a sudden, Jody is no longer this man-child of the house. He becomes more like a little boy. Jody starts complaining to his mom that Melvin (Ving Rhames) is drinking all the Kool-Aid. He's eating the food. I just thought, yeah, he really did seem like a little boy then.

I thought that the character of Melvin was dealt with well because they could have easily made him sort of typical . . . "Oh, he's bad; no, he's good" [type of character]. But they kept a certain complexity because you could tell he wanted to do right, and he was trying to do right, but he was still a violent guy. An O.G. [Original Gangsta], as Jody calls him.

INDU

Yeah, when Melvin's caught growing marijuana amongst the tomatoes out back, he was very good at apologizing. Very smooth.

ACID

I liked the depiction of these two older characters having crazy sex. Like when they're jumping up and down and around the room.

INDU

Yeah. I really enjoyed that. The actress playing the mom in Baby Boy, A.J, Johnson was quite charming.

ACID

Like, I . . . really empathized with her. I really felt her vulnerability; even though she was a tomboy and always rough and tough, I always just felt like she's this far away from losing it. . . . . Any last thoughts on how this female director and this male director portrayed love differently?

INDU

I think in the universe that's portrayed by Love and Basketball, there's just a little bit more compassion and kindness.

ACID

Do you think that John Singleton would have made a better film if Baby Boy would have illustrated more clearer the social machinery that is kind of pushing his characters to act [in] this violent, aggressive way? Would you have empathized with them more? Would you have said, "Okay, I understand, of course," and felt for them?

INDU

I would have liked to see a little bit more contact with the outside world. I know that people live in really self-contained universes, but I would have liked to see some interaction outside of that immediate world.

ACID

There's no white people in Baby Boy. Or Hispanic or Asian.

INDU

Yeah, there was something missing there, like there's a mysterious hand guiding these clearly flawed characters. And I guess the audience is just supposed to go, "Oh, yes, . . . they're obviously down on their luck 'cause they're black and live in South Central," and we're supposed to feel bad for them because these things are happening. But you know, I think that denies something inherent in all people.

ACID

It's weird because I find not just black directors but American directors have a certain myopia when it comes to race, and I swear to God, it feels like if you came from another planet; it feels like America's made up [solely] of black and white people.

3.) (White) Girls Ain't Nothin' But More Trouble

A.) *Guess Who's Coming to Dinner* (1967)

Directed by: Stanley Kramer

Written by: William Rose

Outline: Spencer Tracy and Katharine Hepburn play a white couple whose racial opinions are challenged when their daughter brings home a black fiancé.

With: Spencer Tracy, Sidney Poitier, and Katharine Hepburn

B.) *Black and White* (1999)

Written & Directed by: James Toback

Outline: A cinema veritÈ look at the affect of hip-hop culture on rich white Manhattan kids.

With: Mike Tyson, Scott Caan, Robert Downey Jr., and Allan Houston.

GUESS WHO'S COMING TO DINNER vs BLACK AND WHITE

ACID

Whatta you find totally different?

SWEET BWAOY

The token freaking speeches of the characters in Guess . . . Dinner. It's not so much dialogue, it's . . . like a Martin Luther King speech or something. The movie just took out the best parts of what should've been dramatized and just stuck in the dialogue and then called it a movie.

SASSY AM

It should have come out of the dialogue, out of the staging of the scene, [and] out in the characterizations of people.

ACID

Okay Sweet Bwaoy, you're an aspiring filmmaker — quickly break down Guess Who's Coming To Dinner, 'cause you know Stanley Kramer directed it, and he's respected as one of the legends of directing. Break down the color palette, break down the way the scenes worked for you, break down the script — did it get to you, did the story arcs work, did it flow, was the cinematography there?

SWEET BWAOY

In the beginning, the twist — this black man and white woman being in love — was introduced immediately. Boom. It seems that could've dragged that out a lot more efficiently. They could have made it a little bit more of it and built up some suspense.

ACID

I felt that it should have been plot point one, introduced at about the 20-minute mark instead of right at the opening.

SWEET BWAOY

Yeah, exactly — I think that movie was completely out of order . . . in terms of the order of scenes. Like, when they kicked her out, they shoulda had her cause more havoc, and then in the climax kick her out. Or the mother — [there's] Sidney Poitier's mother, and she's breaking it down to him saying [something like], "Look, you're just a bitter old man who doesn't even remember what it's like to be in love.". That should have been closer to the climax — there were some good scenes, some good acting, but it was all out of order. It was too preachy. It was like a propaganda film.

SASSY AM

And they focused more on the issue of the black man. It's his problem. . . It's not only is a problem between the family who is white and the family who's black, it's just all of a sudden the story focus around black, the color blackÖ What about the color white? What impact does it have on society versus what it has on us? It's always the black people put up front. That's the problem.

SWEET BWAOY

Yeah, there's a line in the freaking script that even said, so what if he [Sidney] has a pigmentation problem.

SASSY AM

Exactly. The minute there's . . . a drop of black or a color put into anything, it becomes a problem, an issue, and that's the focal point of this whole movie. It's not that it's two people coming together, regardless of their background and their race — black is an issue.

You know, we're focusing on the black and white couple here. . . What about the whole thing about love? Love is blind.

ACID

But did you think that the movie got across that these two were in love? Poitier and the white girl, Dr. Prentice and Joey?

SWEET BWAOY

It seemed to me that they had a father-daugh-

ter relationship, that's what I was seeing, man.

SASSY AM

They said they wanted to get married. But there was no real passion.

SWEET BWAOY

Do you think it's poor directing on Stanley Kramer's part? Or do you think he chickened out?

[I think] maybe he chickened out. Think about it- it's the 1960s, he's on the set with a bunch of old white people, and he's gotta tell this black actor to get touchy feely with this white chick.

ACID

I think that there's also a subtext in the casting. The fact [is] that there are three major actors in the leads, but the daughter who's getting married is not a major white actress. Really, I think it says something that she's an unknown, really. Why not put Kim Novak or Elizabeth Taylor in it as the daughter? That would have been controversial.

ACID

Yeah. Now, as far as the movie Black and White and how they dealt with black male/white female sexual dealings.

SASSY AM

I could make a comparison in both films. In

Guess Who's Coming to Dinner, it's always some white-blonde hair, blue eyed, upper-crust girl with the predominant black doctor character — he's educated, he's intelligent, he's making money. So [you can think about] that as being, you know, you need something white on the side to bring you up higher. I think it's a bad reflection on black men . . . for choosing that type of women that they want around them.

SWEET BWAOY

The line in the Sydney Poitier movie where the white girl is like, "Yeah, he's a very important man, and when I marry him, I'll be important, too." Remember that line? That coincides with that line in Black and White where the girl says, "Look, we get with black people for protection." They both want something from these black male characters to elevate them.

ACID

In films it's always black men, white women, that connection. What if the role was reversed and all the movies are about white men macking with black girls? Sassy, what do you feel about the message in Guess Who's Coming to Dinner of this accomplished black man, and there couldn't have been that many in the 60s, that he's drawn to this white woman? How do you feel as a black woman when you watch Sydney Poitier, the quintessential great handsome leading man, mack that white girl?

SASSY AM

I just think he's selling out.

ACID

What about Black and White, how did you feel about the lead character, Richie Bauer, macking on all those white girls?

SASSY AM

I was sick. I was disgusted by it because the film was saying that his purpose was behind using these women — he didn't care about them, he treated them like shit, he talked to them like shit, he played with them. So I have nothing nice to say about. There's no value, there's nothing — it's just crap. It's just a bunch of bullshit.

ACID

Okay. So Sydney Poitier's movie — we agree that for the 60s, it was trying to say something. Now do you think that the ideal — the ideals that they were trying to push forward in Guess Who's Coming To Dinner, the let's-all-get-along theme — has come true today, thirty-five years later?

SASSY AM

What they're trying to do is paint a picture of the black man, being that if he's successful and intelligent, he could get a white woman to admire him and stick with him.

SWEET BWAOY

When you were a little kid, you're getting crushes on a white kid, a black kid, right 'cause you're a kid, and you don't know about the sociopolitical bullshit that goes with it right. I think that's what this movie's kinda dealing with a little bit. For me, it goes back to that line, "You don't know what it's like to be in love."

ACID

Now in Black and White, what they're saying about black and white culture intersecting, do you think that's accurate of what happens in our society?

Like basically, Guess Who's Coming To Dinner is trying to say the races will all come together if we can just accept people not judge them based on skin color. So what is the underlying message in Black and White?

SWEET BWAOY

Black and White is what happens when Look Who's Coming to Dinner finally comes into fruition and then gets horribly out of hand.

SWEET BWAOY

It's the point where everyone [became] accepting of it. It's like in Look Who's Coming to Dinner,

everyone said, 'Okay, fine. We're all human beings here; let's just get along.' And then Black and White is what happens when you take it to the next level and start getting nasty with white chicks with no fear of lynching.

But I'd rather believe in the world of Black and White than live in the world of Look Who's Coming to Dinner.

ACID

As a black person are you offended by some of the subtext?

SASSY AM

No, I'm not offended, I just don't like the style of how the movie was put together back then. It's like some of it was real, [but overall] they didn't deal with the real aspect of the implication of two [people] in that era coming together [in terms of] race. They don't even deal with the family's friends. You know — the relatives, their friends, going to certain department stores or coffee shops that you go by yourself, and now all of a sudden you've got a black man by your side. How are people gonna react?

SWEET BWAOY

I just loved Black and White in terms of how the actors were directed. Not necessarily in terms of the visual aesthetic of it, but just how the actors were directed. I can catch the realness of it. And I'm curious to know how he directed those scenes. I wouldn't be surprised if he shot like millions of feet of . . . film and just like took the best parts.

4.) Damn it Feels Good to be a Gangster

A.) *Belly* (1998)

Directed by: Hype Williams

Written by: Anthony Bodden and Nas

With: DMX, Nas, Tionne 'T-Boz' Watkins, and Louie Rankin.

B.) *The Harder They Come* (1973)

Directed by: Perry Henzell

Written by: Perry Henzell & Trevor D. Rhone

Outline: Ivan, a poor Jamaican country boy, comes to Kingston to seek fame and fortune.

With: Jimmy Cliff, Janet Barkley, Carl Bradshaw, and Ras Daniel Hartman

BELLY vs THE HARDER THEY COME

ACID

So we just checked out the Jamaican classic film The Harder They Come. How'd it play almost 30 years after it was made?

SWEET BWAOY

When I re-examine and watch that film again, it's actually still really good cinema. The very first time I watched it, it was a shitty print. Like, there was parts where you couldn't even see the people, but this time I realize it's actually different in terms of the plot structure, in terms of acting, in terms of, like, everything's actually really good.

ACID

Technically, some of the interior scenes are just not lit — it's ridiculous. But story wise, it's tight. . . . . Each frame is just funky, each looks like it could be a magazine photo.

DON CASH

I was really shocked by how well shot the movie was, and to me, it's very similar to Scorcese's Mean Streets in the grit of the characters and their world. It's just got a real nice feel to it, like maybe like a Cassevetes feel, so it's just . . . cool.

SWEET BWAOY

The plot structure on that is pretty tight. [You've] got the classic set up. This guy Ivan comes out of some situation. In this case it's a grandmother is dead, he's out of the country, he's gotta [go somewhere], and he goes to his mom in the city for help, and initially from the setup, there's conflict. . . . He's a guy with no money, but he's gotta get some money. Some fame.

ACID

I'm reading that Robert McKee book Story About Script Structure, which is excellent. And he says one of the most important things about creating a protagonist is that you have to empathize with him, whether he's a good guy or a bad guy. Not sympathize, but empathize, and I think this script achieves that quite well, right off the bat. It's a classic Greek story — like, he's pushed out into the world by the death of a maternal figure, the death of his grandmother. So he comes to Kingston to tell his mother that the grandmother has died, and rather than receive some love and affection from the mother, she sorta shuns him... His mother just wants to know if there's any money from the death of the grandmother.

So she can't help him. So he's gotta go to, like, the next thing, which is God, you gotta go to the church. He goes to the church, and still, even though he's trying to make something of himself, he meets up with resistance rather than acceptance.

SWEET BWAOY

There is some sort of significance to that scene where Ivan says that famous line: 'Don't fuck with me.' It's like a man who everywhere, he goes wants to agitate, doesn't want to live with the status quo [or] live quietly in his place in the world.

ACID

So me and Sweet Bwaoy have seen Belly before, so you speak first, Don.

DON CASH

It's well shot, it's beautiful — it's a beautiful looking movie — but there's no centre to the movie. This story is completely ludicrous from almost the beginning to the very end. The first ten minutes are good. Then the holes start coming into the narrative. Then those holes start getting bigger and bigger and bigger. So I don't think that it's really possible to talk about this film's significance in hip-hop culture because the plot is just a failure, you know. In some ways, it's kinda symbolic of hip-hop these days in terms of its bling-bling soul, a soul centred on artifice and style to the total detriment of . . . anything that means anything. And the movie just sort of relies on a moral centre that is common to the hip-hop world — you know, a Nation of Islam sort of moralism — to give it some kind of centre. And that's a lot like regular hip-hop these days, you know — no real imagination — so

it's pointing to something in the past to claim that they have some sort of spirituality.

ACID

So without any moral centre, the film lacks any real stakes, and without any real stakes, there's little room for any true drama.

DON CASH

Yeah, so the film is grabbing at straws to make it entertaining. For example, the part with Method Man —you know, showing up after he got shot in the chest with a 12-gauge shotgun earlier in the script.

It seems like probably that part happened at the end of the original script, and then they decided to put it in the middle, because it doesn't make any fuckin' sense. Then the DMX character is shooting some guy, in the middle of the hot spot, the best restaurant in the city! Like I was saying, what kinda gangstas shoot somebody in the middle of a hot restaurant? The whole point of being a gangsta, more than getting the money, is to be slick; it's to go out and be seen in all the best spots. If no one lets you into your club because you're shooting people right in the middle of the fuckin' dining room, what's the point of being a gangsta?

ACID

There's no sense in being a gangsta if you gotta go to McDonalds.

DON CASH

The whole point is you're a gangsta, not a common criminal. The whole point of being a gangsta is that people don't see you killing people, no one knows — to them, it's a buncha lies, . . . 'The Man' just wants to get you. When you're a gangsta, that's the whole point: 'The Man' says you're bad, but you're not really bad, you just have money. But the would-be gangstas in Belly, they're acting like common criminals.

ACID

When I first saw Belly, I guess because everybody had said it was so bad, my expectations were really lowered, and then I saw it and visually just blew me, so I guess the story [was what] I didn't pay attention to because I wasn't expecting much. This sounds ridiculous, but I thought this movie was a classic. I used to big it up to everybody, and now I don't know if it is. And this is about my fourth time seeing it.

SWEET BWAOY

Watching both those movies side by side just shows you that story is the most important [thing] 'cause in terms of visuals, the two movies can't compare. Belly is more beautiful, but you're still more drawn to The Harder They Come. Visuals alone can't keep you there.

SWEET BWAOY

You know what that reminds me of? The original Ocean's Eleven, you seen the original Ocean's Eleven with Frank Sinatra?

It's like Belly. An all-star cast, man — you got frickin' Frank Sinatra, you got Joey Bishop, Sammy Davis Jr. You got Dean Martin. You got all these big stars in a heist movie. And it's the worst movie you ever seen in your life.

DON CASH

Belly's an interesting movie though because you can tell that this is at the end of an era, and the whole hip-hop thing does not matter.

DON CASH

I remember when I was in New York, in 1999 when Belly is set and I remember thinking the exact same thing: Well, hip-hop's dead, thug's dead. Like black people [are] still alive and are gonna be rapping over beats, but the whole hip-hop thing is dead, you know?

SWEET BWAOY

What was the initial tip-off?

DON CASH

There was just something about being in the streets. What really ticked me off was [that] there's a certain energy in the East Village, and then I'd go to Brooklyn and I'd be at the mall, and I'd see all these kids acting tough and everything. I'd be like, you would probably not be acting so tough if you realized that people in Brampton dress like you, look like you, know the same music, everything. So that there's this whole kind of realization happening around the same time that maybe what we're doing isn't as cool as we think [it is]. The whole hip-hop thing had been, like, the coolest thing going for the longest time, and it just reached the point where even though it was really successful and people were making money, it was at the point where you know there's cooler things out there.

It's dead. Hip-hop is never coming back; it's over. It's, like, that's the thing — rap music is gonna be around, but for all intents and purposes, it's gone.

ACID

Spike Lee says he was trying to like say goodbye to. . . the gangsta-b-boys-in-the-hood movies with Clockers. Maybe Hype just said goodbye to rap movies.

5.) (It was) da Best of Times and the Worst of Times

A.) *Wild Style* (1982)

Written and Directed by: Charlie Ahearn

Outline: A run-and-gun docudrama that captures the buzz of the early years of hip-hop's birth in the Bronx.

With: Patti Astor, Fab Five Freddy, and the RockSteady Crew

B.) *Rappin'* (1985)

Directed by: Joel Silberg

Written by: Adam Friedman and Robert Jay Litz

Outline: An ex-con/break-dancer helps his neighborhood battle a greedy land developer.

With: Mario Van Peebles, Kadeem Hardison , and Eriq La Salle

WILD STYLE vs RAPPIN'

ACID

So what do you think [of Rappin'] especially seen next to Wild Style, which was a pretty good rap movie.

BROWN MAN

Pretty good — Wild Style was the real deal. Wild Style is a movie that's very documentary style without being a mocumentary.

Wild Style is just real, I love reality, and Rappin' is such a fuckin' farce.

ACID

So what didn't work with Rappin'? What didn't you like about it?

BROWN MAN

Every fuckin' minute of it. The fact that Mario Van Peebles is in it is a very damn good place to start as to what I didn't like about it. When Mario Van Peebles is the lead of a quote-unquote black film, there's problem ahead.

Like, take the movie Breakin' — it was made by the exact same people who made Rappin'. Golan Globus did Breakin'. And it was corny, right? But because it came out just before Beat Street did, like about a month and a half before Beat Street did, we

loved it, 'cause there was nothing out in the mainstream on rap. There was Wild Style, but that was an underground release.

ACID

Oh really?

BROWN MAN

Yeah. So they got lucky with Breakin' 'cause there was nothing else for rap fans to watch.

They were trying to cash in on hip-hop 'cause they saw the success of Breakin' and Beat Street, and they said okay, let's go to the next level now, and let's go behind the music. Because Breakin' and Beat Street was about the dancing. . . I'm sure that if fuckin' this movie Rappin' was a success, they [would have] done a movie called Graffiti-in'. You know what I mean? Because they woulda just taken every fuckin' element of hip-hop and tried to make a movie about it.

ACID

The four elements of hip-hop?

BROWN MAN

Yeah — MCing, deejaying, b-boying and breakin', and graffiti.

BROWN MAN

If white people had seen that movie — and I'm

sure at some point they did — I believe that's the reason why white people today make fun of hip-hop. Ever hear white people do their imitation of what rap sounds like to them?

ACID
Like the Rappin' Duke?

BROWN MAN
Yeah, like, "I'm goin' to the stoh. Don't bother me no moh." You know what I mean? "Look, I'm rappin'!" You know what I mean? That's because of movies like that, that fuckin' movie Rappin'. When people don't understand the culture or the music, that's what they think it's all about. And now it's at a different level where white people just think you need to say 'motherfucker' and 'nigger'— like, 'I shot a muthafuckah,' and [you've got a] rap record.

6.) I'm So Slack (Black Slackers)

A.) *The Lunatic* (1991)

Directed by: Lol Creme

Written by: Anthony C. Winkler (also novel)

Outline: A Jamaican lunatic falls for a fat German tourist

With: Carl Bradshaw, Paul Campbell, and Julie T. Wallace

B.) *Basquiat* (1996)

Directed by: Julian Schnabel

Written by: Lech Majewski, John F. Bowe

Outline: An indie film that depicts the fall and rise of Jean-Michel Basquiat, the young Hatian graffiti artist who took Andy Warhol's New York Art scene by storm in the 80s

With: Jeffrey Wright, Michael Wincott, Benicio Del Toro, Claire Forlani, and David Bowie

THE LUNATIC vs BASQUIAT

ACID

I've seen The Lunatic quite a few times. I'll go there really quickly, then you comment on Basquiat. The Lunatic is basically about this Jamaian guy who's a lunatic. . . The lunatic is homeless — he lives on a small part of an estate that's owned by a light-skinned, upper-class Jamaican. He calls himsef Alowitious, and he talks to all the inanimate objects in his life: he talks to the trees, he talks to the cricket balls, everything.

Halfway through the film he kind of falls in love with a fat German girl. And the storyline is then about their love affair, and the trouble she gets him into, and . . . it's pretty much a farce, [but] it comments through drama on the society in Jamaica. It comments on the way that power congregates.

Donald Bogle, a black film historian, writes about how a lot of American jazz movies never showed any genuine camaraderie between the black artists. In films like Sweet Love, Bitter, Paris Blues, and A Man Called Adam, they fail to create a sense of community of black artists, jazz musicians. I think that Basquiat is guilty of that as well. I mean Jean Michel, he's from Haiti, but they never showed the Haitian community. It's as if the director, Julian Schnabel, who was a fellow artist of that era, is saying that Basquiat only came into being once the [white] art world acknowledged him. It's an existential slap in the face.

DON CASH

But the film does succeed in presenting a compelling real life black figure. . . You never really see black artists portrayed in that manner, you know — [he was] as clever and avant garde as his white counterparts. . . You just have to look at the cultural legacies of people like Bob Marley or Marvin Gaye or Sly Stone, and then look at the cultural legacy of somebody like John Lennon or Jim Morrison. It's, like, people like John Lennon and Jim Morrison are celebrated as the greatest poets of our time. . . . [What about] people like Marvin Gaye and Sly Stone — nobody is really talking about how great they were.

ACID

You have a certain understanding of the role that critics play in an artist's life, and one thing I thought was interesting was the character of the journalist Rene, who was this art critic who basically discovered Basquiat, or at least he kind of starts to illuminate him, and he's sort of an underground art critic.

DON CASH

I think that they wanted to have a cautionary tale — don't forget the people who brought you up.

But I think, at the same time, everybody knows the game — you know if you meet one person, you get some money. If you start hanging out with these other people, you get a lot more. Rene knows that that's how Jean Michel has to play the game.

Epilogue

In the end, the genesis of Reel Blak came from a basic, almost primal need to be heard by audiences who share our views. We want to have a psychic dialect with them in regards to what we are seeing in the art and information that is presented to us; in fact, we want to express an opinion for everyone possible to hear. In the words of John Ruskin:

"The greatest thing a human soul ever does in this world is to see something and tell what they saw in a plain way . . . to see clearly is poetry, prophecy and religion, all in one."

Reek Blak was some of what I saw.

Appendex - Our Top-Ten Lists

A top-ten film list almost always says more about the person or people creating the list than it says about any definitive merit or failure of the films themselves. Our lists are no different. Many people will disagree with our choices or even with our interpretation of what constitutes an "urban" film, and they could be right. But fuck it. Most films are like fashion - they come in and go out of style on a continual basis. In a few years, our valuations of these films could be totally off. But for at this moment, we stand by our choices.

Top Ten Best Urban Films

1. Do The Right Thing
Universal/MCA (1989)
Directed by Spike Lee
Spike brings America's racial tensions to the boiling point on the hottest day of the summer in a mixed Brooklyn neighborhood.

2. Cyclo
Cinepix (1995)
Directed by Bnh Hung Tran
The director of the Academy Award Nominated film The Scent of Green Papaya delivers a powerful coming-of-age tale of a young cyclo (bicycle-taxi rider) in Ho-Chi-Min-City who gets mixed up with a charming Vietnamese gangster.

3. Salaam Bombay!
Film 4 Int'l (1988)
Directed by Mira Nair
Oliver Twist meets the third world in Salaam Bombay. It's a raw and moving story of the street urchins of Bombay who live a harsh existence of selling tea, but mostly of begging for money and keeping out of the way of brutal police officers.

4. Pixote
Unifilms (1981)
Directed by Hector Babenco
The mean streets of Sau Paulo is the world that our protaganist, the young delinquent Pixote, must navigate to survive. The gritty cinema verité style of this film grips you and doesn't let go as it spins an animalistic tale of a street kids doomed to a life of hell on earth.

5. New Jersey Drive
Gramercy Pictures (1995)
Directed by Nick Gomez
An existential and cinematic meditation of misguided youth "addicted" to the rush of carjacking in Newark, New Jersey, the unofficial car theft capital of the world. Jason and Midget are two black boyz from tha hood who escape the nihilism of their hopeless existence by cruising around in fancy stolen cars. That is, until a violent police force tries to put a stop to the joyride for good.

6. My Favourite Year
MGM (1982)
Directed by Richard Benjamin
Peter O'Toole plays a fading 50s movie star with a thirst for booze in this send-up of the live TV variety shows of the time (e.g. The Sid Caesar Show of Shows). Benjy Stone is the show's aspiring gag writer who is assigned to babysit the wild and wooly star during the week that he is to gueststar on the King Kaiser show. It's a funny and classy love letter to the bygone era of live, seat-of-your-pants TV.

7. Basquiat
Miramax (1996)
Directed by Julian Schnabel
The quirky and charming movie Basquiat cleverly illustrates the meteoric and colorful life of the infamous young Hatian pop artist Jean-Michel Basquiat. Starting out tagging Manhattan with his graffitti and living in Thompkins Square Park in a cardboard box, Jean-Michel is soon discovered by Andy Warhol's art world of the 80s, and Jean becomes its black star. But the price of fame is high as the money and prestige take Basquiat's vices to new heights.

8. Kids
Miramax (1995)
Directed by Larry Clark
A fucked-up slice of teen life in New York City, Clark's controversial movie traces twenty-four hours in the grim life of Telly, a 17-year-old white boy slacker who's on a mission to fuck as many virgins as possible, sans condoms.

When Telly's old girlfriend tests positive for HIV, she chases through New York City to stop him before he fucks again.

9. The Harder They Come
Island Pictures (1973)
Directed by Perry Henzell
When country boy Ivan (Jimmy Cliff) hits the city of Kingston, he's got big dreams of making a hit record. But after he finds out that the record business is wicked, he tries his hand at ganja dealing, only to find out that there is no honour among thieves and that the cops really run things. By the time Ivan kills a cop, his record is a hit on the radio, becoming his theme song while he's a fugitive. It's not long before a hail of police bullets brings Ivan's story to an end, but not before his exploits have made him Jamaica's most wanted man and cult hero to the Jamaican underclass. It is an all too brief glimpse of hope for the oppressed.

10. My Beautiful Laundrette
Orion Classics (1985)
Directed by Stephen Frears
My Beautiful Laundrette is a cautionary parable of the devastating effects of Thatcherism on Britain's slacker class. And despite the laziness of those around him, South Asian immigrant, Omar is out to get his when he gets a chance at his piece of the economic pie by running his Uncle Nasser's laundrette. Omar is helped by his friend Johnny a white Londoner and former classmate. The clash of cultures in this new and changing England is presented with a comic insight into this changing world.

Top Ten Worst Urban Films

1. Can't Stop The Music
EMI films (1980)
Directed by Nancy Walker
Bruce Jenner stars in this ridiculous pseudo biography of the birth of the even more ridiculous band The Village People. Set in Greenwich Village, it sets out to be a celebration of the disco era but is more enjoyable for the wacky gay subtext.

2. Money Train
Columbia Pictures (1995)
Directed by Joseph Ruben
Two unlikely foster brothers (Woody Harrelson and Wesley Snipes) are transit cops with a serious case of sibling rivalry. Hollywood obviously thought they'd strike gold again with the pair, like they did in White Man Can't Jump. No such luck. The premise is promising: the two subway cops decide to rip off the train that carries the transit payroll. Add sexy newcomer Jennifer Lopez and watch the sparks fly. This movie did the opposite. It sunk at the box office and with critics alike.

3. Outta Sync
Live Entertainment (1995)
Directed by Debbie Allen
An absurd would-be thriller that stars LL Cool J as a club disc jockey who is forced by bad cop Howard Hesseman to use his druggie past to get buddie-buddie with a local drug pusher. It shoulda worked - LL as DJ, Dr. Fever as a grizzled cop. It didn't.

4. Def Jam's How to Be a Player
Gramercy Pictures (1997)
Directed by Lionel Martin!
Def Jam artists consistently rock tha mic in the hip-hop world, but the legendary label really slipped with this movie. Bill Bellamy stars as Dray, a young playboy who's out to mack every fine girl he scopes. Bellamy is a charming and funny actor, but that's all subverted for the sake of blatant crude sexcapades. It's like an extended booty video outta control.

5. Slaves of New York
TriStar/Columbia (1989)
Directed by James Ivory
Tama Janowitz' supposed hip and avant garde novel of the same name gets the once over by Merchant/Ivory and their star Bernadette Peters. It's still a mystery why the duo known for upper-crust snoozers like A Room With a

View even took this on. And Bernadette Peters is about as downtown as Carol Channing.

6. *Def by Temptation*
Directed by James Bond III
This is a pretty bad neo-blaxploitation would-be horror film about a sexy but evil succubus out to get her feed on horny NYC brothers. The movie's got great actors like Sam Jackson and Bill Nunn, but the poor script and cheapo production value make this film a bore.

7. *Straight Outta Brooklyn*
Samuel Goldwyn Co. (1991)
Directed by Matty Rich
Why this debut got so much positive recognition is a head scratcher. Sure, the back story of how untrained filmmaker Matty Rich used an incredible amount of will power to make a feature film is admirable, but when the lights go down and you judge what's on the screen, you'll realize it's kinda crappy. It's especially bad in light of such great films like Menace II Society and New Jersey Drive, which dealt with similar issues and themes.

8. *London Kills Me*
Polygram Filmed Entertainment (1991)
Directed by Hanif Kureishi
Hanif Kureishi is the writer responsible for writing the great film My Beautiful Laundrette. I guess the Oscar nomnation that he got for that went to his head, and he decided he could direct. Wrong! The depressing story follows a hard luck victim of Thatcherism (again) as he tries to escape London's drug world by getting a job as a waiter. He's gotta come up with a "proper pair of shoes" to keep the job, so that's what we see - some meandering, metaphoric journey to find some shoes in London. Ken Loach did Brit-misery much better in Raining Stones.

9. *Drop Squad*
Gramercy Pictures (1994)
Directed by David C. Johnson
An unfunny alleged political satire about an underground militant group of black guys and girls who kidnap and deprogram Uncle Toms. The movie's a mess from the get-go. It's unfortunate because the issue of sell-out sin in the black community is a deliciously loaded one. But despite an excellent cast including Ving Rhames and Eriq LaSalle, the movie isn't really worth watching.

10. D.C. Cab
Universal Pictures (1983)
Directed by Joel Schumacher
It's about hapless cabbies and a rundown cab company in D.C. It stars Mr. T, is directed by the guy who did Car Wash, and is set in the early 80s. 'Nuff said. It's really bad.

Top Ten Most Underrated Urban Films

1. Hav Plenty
Miramax (1997)
Directed by Chris Scott Cherot
Chris Cherot's debut is a cerebral romantic comedy that never got the props it deserved. Cherot plays Lee Plenty, an almost-broke would-be novelist who against his better judgment finds himself falling for the bitchy but sexy-as-hell Haviland Savage during a down-and-out New Year's Eve weekend. Hav is a friend from university who, unlike Lee, has managed to get into the money-making rat-race. Though the low budget is apparent, Cherot creates probably the most twisted and complex young black male character we've ever seen in American cinema.

2. Crooklyn
Universal Pictures (1994)
Directed by Spike Lee
Spike's cinematic slice of childhood nostalgia is deliciously lensed by the excellent AJ Jaffa (Daughters of the Dust) and is one of the best and most complete stories that Spike has ever created. The performances of Delroy Lindo and Alfre Woodard will make you weep, and the

soundtrack will make you reminisce. Fuck Boogie Nights - Crooklyn is what the 70s were really about for a lot of us.

3. *Belly*
Artisan (1998)
Directed by Hype Williams
Rap-video-maker extraordinaire Hype Williams once said that he made hip-hop look more intelligent than it was. I believe him. This movie made headlines when it was released because Magic Johnson refused to carry it in his very lucrative West Coast cinema complex, a death blow for a black film. Critics and audiences dissed the movie for its weak story and extreme violence, but in retrospect, it works as a lush photogenic capturing of the death of crystal- and platinum-hued hip-hop. Sure the story is all over the place, but so is hip-hop. And DMX is truly riveting as a lost soul. The Jamaica sequence is the most stunning bit of film in any hip-hop movie.

4. *Tougher Than Leather*
New Line Cinema (1988)
Directed by Rick Rubin
This Run DMC movie made two crucial mistakes. First of all, it's legal problems kept it out of cinemas initially, and by the time it was released, Run DMC was old news. Had it been released at Run DMC's height of popularity (somewhere between the Raising Hell and Tougher than Leather albums), it woulda been a hit. Secondly, it was released while the rap world still took itself too seriously. Sure Rick Rubin's neophyte directing skills are crap, and the story and plotting are crap, too. But c'mon - it's Run Dmc. The legendary Run DMC. Besides, it's better than any Elvis movie, and they're looked on as cult classics.

5. *Lift* (unreleased)
Directed by DeMane Davis & Khari Streeter
This feature made the film fest circuit in 2000 and 2001, but inexplicably it never found a distributor. Granted it's rough around some of it's edges, but this clever cinematic allegory about the world of Afro-American "boosters," or shoplifters, is fresh, enjoyable, and deserves to be seen. The protagonist Niecy, a charismatic, intelligent young female booster, tries in vain to smooth over her family's dysfunctionality with constant gifts of stolen Gucci and Prada. In the end, as always, crime don't pay. Better yet, Lift doesn't progress to an obvious and clichéd climax. Rather, it really lets the characters resonate. It's a solid and funky drama.

6. *Mixing Nia*
Xenon Entertainment (1998)
Directed by Alison Swan
This debut film by director Alison Swan should-
da been as financially well received as the
other black romantic comedies that followed
in the next two years. Mixing Nia is just as
good as The Best Man, The Brothers, etc., but
for some reason it didn't get to make the
rounds in the Atlanta, DC, Silver Springs' mul-
tiplexes.

The title character Nia is played to virginal
perfection by The Fresh Prince's Karyn
Parsons. She's a hot Manhattan copywriter
who acts white though her mom's black. She
has a crisis of conscience and quits the
agency rather than push a new brand of beer
to black ghetto kids. This epiphany sets her
off on a journey of self-discovery, which, of
course, includes getting her first black
boyfriend to find out who she really is. In the
end, the movie's message is simple: just be
yourself. The romance is appealing and genuinely funny.

7. *Sankofa*
Mypheduh Films (1993)
Directed by Haile Gerima
Sankofa is obviously not an urban film. But
simply put, every black person should see this
film. It should be the cinematic equivalent of
the Alex Haley novel Roots. Every family
should own a copy. The set-up is simple, but
the ramifications elaborate. A stuck-up black
American fashion model on a photo shoot in
Africa finds herself mysteriously transported
back to a plantation in the West Indies during
slavery times. Here she comes face to face
with the physical and psychic horrors of slavery. Just to make things interesting, Dub Poet
Mutabaruka shows up as her Nat-Turner-like
lover. Soon our model-turned-Kizzy is caught
up in a Maroon-led rebellion. It's the only
black film to tackle the slavery issue on a real
visceral level, and it works.

8. *Devil in a Blue Dress*
Columbia/TriStar (1995)
Directed by Carl Franklin
It's post-war LA, and "Easy" Rawlins is doing
what he can to keep making the payments on
his house. Easy is Walter Mosley's well-known
black private dick from his novels. Denzel
plays the World War II veteran who takes on a
gig to find a missing white woman assumed

119

to be hiding somewhere in LA's black community. Carl Franklin's talent rang true in his debut One False Move, and it still rings true here. Don Cheadle as the trigger-happy country boy is worth the price of admission alone. Again, a great black film that didn't find the big audience that it deserved. It deserves a second look.

9. *Baby Boy*
Columbia/TriStar (2001)
Directed by John Singleton
With Baby Boy, Singleton takes us back to where it all began, in the South Central neighborhood of Ricky and Doughboy, of Tre and Furious Styles. But rather than being an update on that generation, it looks at the present boy in that 'hood generation.

The baby boy of the title is Jody (Tyrese Gibson), an unemployed young black man who at twenty is still living with his mother though he's got two baby mamas of his own. Things start to ruffle Jody's "perfect lifestyle" when mom gets a man, an OG (Original Gangsta) played simmeringly by a thugged-out Ving Rhames. And if that wasn't bad enough, he ticks off a gang-banga, creepily played by Snoop Dog, who's now out gunnin' for him. But even with all this drama, the scariest thing facing Jody is the fact that he must grow up.

This movie is all about the performances, and Singleton does a stellar job with his young ensemble, especially r&b'er Tyrese as Jody. There is such a genuineness to this movie that it plays like a glossy documentary at times. The absurdity of Baby Boy's situation plays its double edge perfectly, being both laugh-out-loud funny and bawl-out sad at the same time.

10. *Chameleon Street Fox Lorber*
Directed by Wendel B. Harris Jr.
Wendel B. Harris Jr. based his film on the real life exploits of two Midwest black conmen, William Douglas Street, Jr. and Erik Dupin, and what he is able to create within that narrative vessel has more to do with Doystefsky than Detroit. William Douglas Street is brilliant and bored, and with his gifted mind being left unchallenged, it gets him into trouble. Harris' production values are nil, but his script and his performance as Street creates one of the richest black movie characters to ever come along. Street's slick mind allows him to impersonate everyone - reporter to doctor to lawyer - all with no real credentials. It's like a trickster Brer Rabbit tale set up

north. Even more subversive is the underlying
message that black America must go to ridiculous lengths to be in the "game" and make
some money.

#	Film	Director	Released	Genra	Length
1.	*8 Mile*	Curtis Hanson	(2002)	drama	110 mins
2.	*Ali*	Michael Mann	(2001)	drama	156 mins
3.	*Always Outnumbered*	Michael Apted	(1998)	drama	104 mins
4.	*American Love Story, An*		(1998)	doc.	300 mins
5.	*Antoine Fisher Story, The*	Denzel Washington	(2002)	drama	100mins
6.	*Asientos*	Francois Woukache	(1996)	drama	52 mins
7.	*Baby Boy*	John Singleton	(2001)	drama	129 mins
8.	*Babymother*	Julian Henriques	(1998)	musical/drama	82 mins
9.	*Back in the Days*	Dewey Thompson	(1993)	short/drama	3 mins
10.	*Bad Boys*	Michael Bay	(1995)	action	126 mins
11.	*Bamboozled*	Spike Lee	(2001)	satire	135 mins
12.	*Basquiat*	Julian Schnabel	(1996)	biopic/drama	108 mins
13.	*Beat Street*	Stan Lathan	(1984)	musical/drama	106 mins
14.	*Belly*	Hype Williams	(1998)	action	95 mins
15.	*Big Momma's House*	Raja Gosnel	(2000)	comedy	98 mins
16.	*Black & White*	James Toback	(2000)	drama	100 mins
17.	*Brown Sugar*	Rick Famuyiwa	(2002)		109 mins
18.	*Bulworth*	Warren Beatty	(1998)	comedy/satire	107 mins
19.	*Can't Stop The Music*	Nancy Walker	(1980)	musical/comedy	118 mins
20.	*Chameleon Street*	Wendel B. Harris Jr.	(1991)	drama/satire	95 mins
21.	*Clockers*	Spike Lee	(1995)	urban/drama	129 mins
22.	*Coffy*	Jack Hill	(1973)		91 minutes
23.	*Concrete Garden, The*	Arlick Riley	(1994)	short drama	23 mins
24.	*Cotton Comes to Harlem*	Ossie Davis	(1970)		97 minutes
25.	*Crooklyn*	Spike Lee	(1994)	drama	115 mins
26.	*Curtis' Charm*	John L'euyer	(1995)	drama	74 mins
27.	*Cyclo*	Bnh Hung Tran	(1995)	urban/drama	120 mins
28.	*Darker Side of Black*	Isaac Julien	(1993)	doc.	55 mins

#	Film	Director	Released	Genra	Length
29.	*DC Cab*	Joel Schumacher	(1983)	comedy	99 mins
30.	*Def by Temptation*	James Bond III	(1990)	horror	95 mins
31.	*Devil in a Blue Dress*	Carl Franklin	(1995)	drama	102 mins
32.	*Do The Right Thing*	Spike Lee	(1989)	urban/drama	120 mins
33.	*Dr. Doolittle*	Betty Thomas	(1998)	comedy	85 mins
34.	*Dr. Doolittle 2*	Steve Carr	(2001)	comedy	87 mins
35.	*Drop Squad*	D. Clark Johnson	(1994)	comedy/satire	86 mins
36.	*Drumline*	Charls Stone III	(2002)	comedy	125 mins
37.	*Eve's Bayou*	Kasi Lemmons	(1997)	drama	109 mins
38.	*Formula 51*	Ronny Yu	(2001)		92 mins
39.	*From Hell*	the Hughes Brothers	(2001)	drama	121 mins
40.	*Glass Shield, The*	Charles Burnett	(1994)	drama	109 mins
41.	*Great Day in Harlem, A*	Jean Bach	(1995)	doc.	60 mins
42.	*Guess Who's Coming To Dinner*	Stanley Karmer	(1967)	drama	108 mins
43.	*Half Past Dead*	Don Michael Paul	(2002)	action	98 mins
44.	*Harder They Come, The*	Perry Henzell	(1973)	drama	120 mins
45.	*Hav Plenty*	Chris Scott Cherot	(1997)	romantic/comedy	84 mins
46.	*He Got Game*	Spike Lee	(1998)	drama	136 mins
47.	*Hell Up in Harlem*	Larry Cohen	(1973)	action	94 mins
48.	*Hoodlum*	Bill Duke	(1997)	drama	130 mins
49.	*Hoop Dreams*	Steve James	(1994)	doc.	170 mins
50.	*How to Be a Player*	Lionel C. Martin	(1997)	comedy	93 mins
51.	*I Spy*	Betty Thomas	(2002)	comedy	96 mins
52.	*In Too Deep*	Michael Rymer	(1999)	drama	95 mins
53.	*Karmen*	Joseph Ramaka	(2002)	drama	86 mins
54.	*Kids*	Larry Clark	(1995)	drama	91 mins
55.	*Le Franc*	Djibril Diop Mambety	(1994)	comedy	44 mins
56.	*Lesson Before Dying, A*	Joseph Sargeant	(1999)	drama	105 mins

#	Film	Director	Released	Genra	Length
57.	*Lethal Weapon 4*	Richard Donner	(1998)	action	127 mins
58.	*Life & Debt*	Stephanie Black	(2001)	doc.	80 mins
59.	*Lift*	Khari Streeter/Demane Davis	(unreleased/2001)	drama	80 mins
60.	*London Kills Me*	Hanif Kureishi	(1991)	drama	107 mins
61.	*Love & Basketball*	Gina Prince-Blythewood	(2000)	drama	124 mins
62.	*Lunatic, The*	Lol Creme	(1991)	comedy	93 mins
63.	*Mandela*	Angus Gibson	(1996)	documentary	60 mins
64.	*Mixing Nia*	Alison Swan	(1998)	romantic/comedy	92 mins
65.	*Money Train*	Joseph Ruben	(1995)	action	103 mins
66.	*My Beautiful Laundrette*	Stephen Frears		drama	97 mins
67.	*My Favourite Year*	Richard Benjamin	(1982)	comedy	92 mins
68.	*New Jersey Drive*	Nick Gomez	(1995)	drama	98 mins
69.	*Once...When We Were Colored*	Tim Reid	(1996)	drama	115 mins
70.	*Out of Sync*	Debbie Allen	(1995)	drama	105 mins
71.	*Panther*	Mario Van Peebles	(1995)	drama	123 mins
72.	*Pearl Harbor*	Michael Bay	(2001)	epic	183 mins
73.	*Pixote*	Hector Babenco	(1981)	drama	122 mins
74.	*Raisin' Kane Rapumentary*	Alison Duke	(2001)	documentary	73 mins
75.	*Rappin'*	Joel Silberg	(1985)	drama	92 mins
76.	*Remember the Titans*	Boaz Yakin drama	(2002)		113 mins.
77.	*Rush Hour II*	Brett Ratner	(2001)	action	90 mins
78.	*Saar*	Selina Williams	(1994)	short drama	28 mins
79.	*Salaam Bombay!*	Mira Nair	(1988)	drama	113 mins
80.	*Sankofa*	Haile Gerima	(1993)	drama	124 mins
81.	*Season of Change, A*	Robert Gervais and Michael Kronish		doc.	
82.	*Show, The*		(1995)		92 mins

#	Film	Director	Released	Genra	Length
83.	*Sidney's Chair*	Robert Bangura	(1995)	short drama	21 mins
84.	*Slaves of New York*	James Ivory	(1989)	comedy	121 mins
85.	*Soul Survivors*	Sandy Johnson	(1995)	comedy	180 mins
86.	*Standing in the Shadows of Motown*				
87.	*Straight Outta Brooklyn*	Matty Rich	(1991)	drama	86 mins
88.	*Sunset Park*	Steve Gomer	(1996)		99 mins
89.	*Tougher Than Leather*	Rick Rubin	(1988)	action	
90.	*Training Day*	Antoine Fuqua	(2001)	drama	120 mins
91.	*Unbreakable*	M. Night Shyamalan	(2000)	thriller	106 mins
92.	*Vampire in Brooklyn*	Wes Craven	(1995)	horror	100 mins
93.	*Vie Sur Terre, La*	Abderrahmane Sissako	(1998)	drama	61 mins
94.	*Vintage*	Thomas Allen Harris		documentary	72 mins
95.	*Watermelon Woman, The*	Cheryl Dunye	(1996)	drama	90 mins
96.	*When Stars Meet the Sea*	Raymond Rajaonarivelo -	(1996)	drama	86 mins
97.	*White Man's Burden*	Desmond Nakano	(1995)	drama	189 mins
98.	*Wild Style*	Charlie Ahearn	(1982)	drama	82 mins
99.	*Wild Wild West*	Barry Sonnenfeld	(1999)	action	107 mins
100.	*Woubi Cherry*	Phillip Brooks	(1998)	documentary	62 mins
101.	*Kirikou & the Sorcereress*	Michel Ocelot	(1998)	animation	74 mins